THE WORDS OF MY MOUTH

Covering the period 1938---2010

Michael Chering

A Bright Pen Book

Copyright © Michael Chering 2010

All rights reserved. No part of this publication may be reproduced, stored in a retrieval system, or transmitted in any form or by any means, electronic, mechanical, photocopy, recording or otherwise, without prior written permission of the copyright owner. Nor can it be circulated in any form of binding or cover other than that in which it is published and without similar condition including this condition being imposed on a subsequent purchaser.

British Library Cataloguing Publication Data.
A catalogue record for this book is available from the British Library

ISBN 978-07552-1368-9

Authors OnLine Ltd
19 The Cinques
Gamlingay, Sandy
Bedfordshire SG19 3NU
England

This book is also available in e-book format, details of which are available at www.authorsonline.co.uk

Introduction

It is some considerable time since I started to write a record of my experiences since my birth in 1938. I suppose I was encouraged to do this as a result and in response to several suggestions made by friends and certain members of the family. For a long time, I was reluctant to do this as I would not consider myself a writer in the sense I could write novels etc. None-the-less the idea grew on me, born out of some of my experiences. I grew to realise that, if I could share some of these moments in my life, that would help to answer many questions in the lives of those who are affected by birth defects and accidents or indeed the result of war damage to themselves or their friends, then this might just help them to know how to overcome these difficulties.

There are so many different aspects to this problem of overcoming and moving on from the traumatic experiences that life brings upon some individuals and groups. It is often quite difficult to know where to begin to give any guidance as to how to advise people without knowing the history of how they came to experience some of these traumas. Once this is known, then we can perhaps make some sense of the situation and give the appropriate help.

I will share with the reader some detail of my experience

from birth right up to my present age. It was not an easy journey by any means. I hope that what I share will be of help to you. I am only a normal every-day sort of chap, with no particular strong point to shout about, but, despite this, I can tell you that many of the experiences I came through were only possible because of the help I received along the way. I will explain how this was made possible in my story.

My hope is that you will be encouraged to overcome any difficulties that you are experiencing by reading this account. I feel that, if I can move on in my life, having in mind the journey I have taken, then you can. Even if after reading this introduction, you may feel it is all a bit fanciful, read the story anyway, it just might inspire you, I hope it does.

Contents

	Introduction	iii
Chapter 1	Early life	1
Chapter 2	School-days	13
Chapter 3	Turning-Point	28
Chapter 4	Teens and Twenties Challenge	38
Chapter 5	The real world of communication	52
Chapter 6	Learning to trust	65
Chapter 7	Speaking Up	78
Chapter 8	Further Challenges	92
Chapter 9	Amazing Grace	106
Chapter 10	The Point of it all	119
	My Positive Conclusion	129

Chapter 1

Early Life

In my introduction, I explained the circumstances of my entrance into this world. Now I move on to cover the period of young childhood to about the age of eight.

I must have been about two years old when I first saw Dr McIndoe and, hard as it may be to believe, I actually remember something of that first meeting. My first impression at that age was someone in a white coat, who looked like anybody's granddad, with a kindly smile and a soft re-assuring way of speaking to me. I also recall seeing lots of people standing around my cot looking at me. My mother told me later that all I could do was cry.

Over the next year the doctors were to be mainly concerned with the corrective work of the operations carried out following my birth. My top lip had begun to come apart again - this is why I could not be fed using a teat in the normal way. Feeding became a matter of urgency. This repair work took about three months, so my mum told me. Mum and Dad appreciated what Dr McIndoe was doing, especially in the circumstances of the war which was producing more and more casualties that needed Dr McIndoe's attention. All this resulted in a heavy demand for the doctor's time and expertise. Other doctors were covering different areas of work, but in the cases where plastic surgery was needed, the team headed by Dr McIndoe, who were specialists in this field, dealt with the more serious cases. So many doctors were on a steep learning curve in those demanding days of trauma.

In those days hare-lip cases were dealt with on a more gradual step-by-step basis in order to take into consideration natural growth and development of the area affected. This was considered the best practice at the time. Nowadays, however, dependent on the case, the operation is done in one or two stages and great strides of progress have been made in this type of surgery since. Many doctors will still say, even today, "It is better to make haste slowly in the more serious cases." Among the reasons given are that the cosmetic results are more acceptable and the speech develops better, with the consonant sounds more distinct. There are differences of approach even among doctors, but for myself, through my experience, the 'make haste slowly' approach has proved best.

For those who may be interested, I have had some 23 operations, including any corrective surgery that became necessary and the dental treatment of later years. It seems quite a lot, but when you consider what the problems were when I was born, you can understand why this was all necessary.

I suppose one has to remember that when I was born, plastic surgery was still in its infancy and the doctors were in a pioneering mode as far as this type of surgery was concerned. I, perhaps was an involuntary 'guinea pig'; I was in no position to argue one way or another. With the benefit of hindsight, I'm glad I didn't know very much about it, except for the pain following operations. They kept my parents informed at each step along the way.

With the benefit of hindsight, again, I'm glad that my treatment was gradual for so many reasons. I am grateful to the doctors who were so patient with me! From a little boy who didn't know what was going on, or why I should be different from everyone else, to coming to realise, as I grew older, that these people were making a big difference in my life. Especially with all the decisions that had to be made as to the next stage of the operations. There were times when I seemed to be surrounded by people in white coats - doctors and students learning about the nature of this type of treatment of people with my sort of problems. From my perspective at the time, white coats seemed to be coming from all directions, but they played a very important part in my life. The foundational operations were to become pivotal to the ultimate success of future operations, this was why it was important to make haste slowly.

Up to this point, no photos were taken of me by my family. The only photos taken were of a medical nature for the use of the surgeons. At four to six years of age impressions are very strong, you become acutely aware of your surroundings and the people around you and what is happening to one. My experience when I was four was of pain in my face and the lack of the ability to eat properly as the doctors carried out operations to repair my mouth. My face seemed always to be bandaged up and I wanted them to take the bandages off! I couldn't understand what was going on as I saw other patients, including children, around me enjoying their food - why couldn't I eat what they were eating? I thought. Of course! I couldn't have that kind of food because I couldn't have managed it. But you try telling a four-year old that! I couldn't ask because I couldn't speak, having no roof to my mouth didn't help. I was probably a frustrated little monkey, with a few tantrums thrown in for good measure.

When I look back, I marvel at the patience, if you forgive the pun, of the nurses who were trying to do their best for me. I could hear what other children in the ward were saying, although I was not in a position to be able to answer them. I didn't look the same as other children. But that is where the difference ended. I could still indicate my approval or otherwise of what was going on. If I was unhappy about something, I could certainly make it known to those around me!

Speech in young children normally begins around the age of nine months to just over a year, just by uttering small words like "mummy" or "daddy", but I could not even manage those words until much later when they would sound like grunts or a cry.

At the age of four I was in Bart's Hospital in London. My parents had to take me by bus or train from Tottenham for appointments. Only one parent would take me as they could not afford two lots of fares. This was not an easy time for them having to cope with the war conditions of 1942. They were worried about air-raids and the like. There were four other children at home between the ages of six and twelve, all needing attention and protection from danger, so the whole thing was fraught with uncertainty. Despite my special needs, I still had to wait my turn for attention. Mum would tell me what was happening at home when she visited the hospital during the times of my operations. This went on for another three years off and on.

Some time during 1944 I was transferred to East Grinstead's Queen Victoria Hospital and my parents could not visit me so often due to the cost of getting there. Conditions at this hospital were slightly better than the inner London Bart's Hospital, due to the damage caused by bombs not being so devastating; London was obviously the main target by the German air-force during 1941-2. I came to realise that the authorities had done a fantastic job in the running of Bart's under such adverse conditions. They had to cope with all casualties in that part of the London area. At the same time I was receiving all the treatment that I needed, amazing! On the other hand, although East Grinstead area was not so badly affected, it had its problems as did other areas outside London.

Queen Victoria Hospital was dealing with people from the armed forces mainly and more particularly the pilots who were shot down and naval people who received severe burns to their bodies which needed expert attention. There was a special ward called 'Canadian Wing', this is the ward I was transferred to. My parents were quite amazed! The reason was because of the nature of plastic surgery I would need as time went on. This 'Canadian Wing' was later famous for the name it was given, which was called 'The Guinea Pig Club', apparently it was given this name because often patients who were in the course of their treatment would visit the local inn and share stories of their experiences and their on-going treatment, They would say that they were just 'guinea-pigs' receiving treatment to see if it would work, this was just a light-hearted way of dealing with their situation. Of course, the treatment did work by-and-large.

Having been placed in such a ward where all these very brave men were receiving treatment, there was always the possibility of me seeing those who had very traumatic injuries and looked quite shocking to the uninitiated, so I was placed in such a position as not to be able to see these patients. They tended to be placed in cubicles on their own, out of sight, in the interest of everyone. I'm sure this must had been appreciated by the patients in question. At my tender age I was very much aware of the impressions given by spotting the more serious cases, and I did on occasion by mistake. I shall never forget what I have seen! But you know, some of these patients demonstrated a remarkable spirit of courage and perseverance in spite of their condition.

The difference all this made to me over time was to realise that no matter what I was feeling about my looks and speech, and how I was to face the world, these people showed me the way I was to handle it. They showed remarkable resilience in the face of tremendous odds stacked against them and I began to feel it was a privilege to be associated with them. Although I didn't realise it at the time, this experience was to affect the rest of my life and still continues to do so at 72. I believe that there is nothing ever completely lost when we consider experiences; they are there to help us along the way. I began to realise, even at my young age then, that despite the way I looked, I was very fortunate.

By the time I was six years old, I was still going in and out of this hospital for operations. I used to get bored on occasion, so I would ask the nurses if I could help them with anything. So I was given some 'little jobs' to help them with, like making the beds, changing linen, and getting water bottles for patients that needed them, those in the ward only, not the cubicles, as I have said. There was a limit to all this because I was not very tall yet. This all helped me no-end, because I didn't have time to get bored any longer, and it helped take my mind off the operations.

Then, one day, the authorities were talking about me making a start on my education. In those days children would start school at five years of age. In my case I was already age six. I was told of the plans to send me to the hospital school. I was really afraid because I knew nobody, I couldn't speak, my face hurt, and I wanted my mum! It was difficult for my family to visit me all the way from Tottenham, because in 1944 the war was still going on and money was tight for my family so I got a visit about once a week. They had quite a job of persuading me to give school a try, not that I had any choice in the matter. As it turned out, it wasn't too bad and I soon started to settle down. My difficulty was communicating with others. Why wasn't I the same as other children there? Why did they stare at me ?

I had so many questions going on in my mind at the time. I couldn't understand what was going on, it was all very confusing! Eventually I came to understand the answers to these questions, but it all took time. I wanted to know the answers then!

My seventh birthday came and went. Britain was still at war, but things were coming to a head. The allies had invaded Normandy in 1944; it was a decisive move and everyone was hoping that the war would soon come to an end. The next operation that I was about to undergo would potentially be just as decisive in the world of my experience. The doctors were going to start to build up a palate/roof to my mouth (palate construction) so I would eventually be able to eat normally and be able to learn to speak more clearly. Whilst I looked forward to being able to do the things that others did automatically, I would have to learn all this from scratch. I was not looking forward to the operations because they would be painful and would take time to heal. I needed a lot of encouragement from everybody to get through this particular phase of operations as they would be vital in any progress that I was to make. Of course, they didn't put it like that; at my age at the time, I was too young to understand the implications of what they were going to do. I mean to say! How do you explain things like this to a child of that age? It took several months to carry out these operations, and they all had to have time to heal first before each stage. Looking back though, I remember that at the time, it seemed ages and ages for them to complete the work. It's probably the worst period for me that I was to cope with! Firstly, I was old enough to know what they were doing, and, secondly, I was more aware of the pain associated with these operations.

Eventually things improved and after some time I was encouraged to try to eat more solid food. As for the speech, this would take some considerable time to develop as after each operation the shape of my palate would be altered, so I had to 'unlearn' some of the ways I got into in trying to talk. I would have to start all over again. The only people that could understand me were my parents to some degree and my sister Betty, she spent the most time with me during the process of learning to speak again. This had to be repeated several times as further operations were carried out. The only way I could communicate with others was to gesticulate in my efforts to make myself understood, and this was difficult, especially when I was at school. The teachers could only look at my written work in order to assess any progress in my understanding of what they were trying to teach.

By the time I was eight I'd got used to the sight of all the 'white coats' milling around watching, looking and listening to me trying to talk, at the same time, looking at each other and making comments, which I didn't understand, obviously trying to assess any progress that I was making.

Also at the same time pulling faces at me to make me laugh. This was largely to establish the way my facial features would move. I didn't realise this at the time though! It's amazing how many muscles one uses when laughing or crying. The doctors would judge the level of progress being made in my profile in this process. This information would be used in future operations to improve my top lip and nasal profile. At eight years old I was becoming more conscious of the way I looked compared with other children of my age, I began to feel very self-conscious about my looks - largely because of the way other children reacted when they looked at me. I often felt upset and depressed about it. I used to confide in the doctors and nurses about my feelings, they would do their best to re-assure me by saying "When you've finished all the treatment, then you will look the same as other people". I knew I had a long way to go before this would happen. When you're young, you want things to happen quickly, don't you? It seemed to me to be such a long time before I could go out and lift my head up without feeling embarrassed and without feeling like a freak amongst others.

So the treatment went on and on, or so it seemed at the time. I came to see more of Dr McIndoe than my own father and mother. He would sit me on a trolley in front of a room full of student doctors and others, all learning about the treatment of this kind of surgical case, which had proved such a challenge over the years. Dr McIndoe always tried to explain in a way that I could understand what he was going to do next. He was very kind and patient with me and easy to talk to. I grew to have complete confidence in him. The operations that he had completed up to this point were all successful. There were many questions in my mind, but I could not make myself understood sufficiently to ask him, but somehow he knew what I was trying to say.

Some people are a bit strange in their reactions to the unusual, and particularly in my case where I had a definite disfigurement. From their point of view they thought I would be a bit soft in the head as well. I suppose if I was in their position I would possibly have come to the same conclusion, not realising the medical wherewithal and prognosis as to the future of such an unfortunate individual.

All this reaction in others didn't help me much at that point in my life though! With hindsight, I didn't have much to worry about. Isn't hindsight a wonderful thing!

My biggest fear when attending school was naturally the attitude of my peers when facing them. As you know, children can be very cruel, especially when they see anyone with any sort of disfigurement or impediment or look different to themselves. They almost cannot help themselves in taking the rise by name calling, abuse or bullying, especially when with their friends in a group.

One trait I was to develop was a sense of self-preservation. I'd come from a big family of nine including my parents, my two other sisters had been added to the family since the end of the war. In a sense I was becoming hard and would stand up to these taunts coming from those at school and in the street. Then something happened which was to have tremendous repercussions for the foreseeable future! I started going to a different sort of school; a Sunday school. This was held at a Mission Hall down the road from where I lived.

This would be a completely new experience for me, one which will be a constant means of reference on so many occasions when relating experiences during the rest of my life. It was to be at this particular place that I was to learn about being accepted and loved by others for who I was. It was to be in complete contrast to the way I was treated at school and in the street generally. I actually looked forward to going to this place where the people were so friendly and kind to me - no name calling, no bullying or making fun of me because of the way I looked. This was refreshing and very encouraging. I was only eight going on for nine at the time and I was very impressionable and sensitive about the way people were treating me at this time.

In chapter two I will talk more about my school-days and experiences.

Chapter 2

School Days

This Sunday school was run by the London City Mission, and I think the reason why my parents sent us (including two older brothers) there, was that they just wanted a bit of quiet on a Sunday morning, not because they had any desire for us to get any religious education to any degree or attachment to a particular faith. Although my father had come from Jewish stock, he did not follow their teaching and had become disinclined to keep the tradition up. Mum was not bothered either way. So we were free to go, more or less, where we wanted, just as long as we were out of a Sunday morning! Little did they realise what a blessing this was to prove to become for me personally. Anyway, we were happy to spend an hour at this place and found that we could have lots of fun there, as we met other kids. Although we were not supposed to be having so much fun, but there to learn about God and Jesus, things like that! To me, at first, it was just like a spill-over from school but before long I began to settle down and take an interest in what was going on. What made it easier for me, is that they were a nice bunch of people and they seemed to have a lot of patience with me and all my troubles in trying to communicate with them. The teachers were very good to me and so were the friends I made at the

Mission hall. They arranged a number of activities. We had a junior club during the week, and we would often go out on outings together, or have a party occasionally. I used to look forward to these occasions, they were in stark contrast to my experience when attending ordinary day school. I started to make some real friends, although I did have a lot of trouble being able to speak to them in a way that they could understand me. I would often get very frustrated. It wasn't because I couldn't think of the words to say, it's just that I couldn't say them! But the Mission people seemed to have so much patience with me in trying to understand what I was saying. It would not be until I was nearly 21 years old, after many more operations and speech-therapy that I would be able to speak in such a way that I could make myself understood more clearly.

The features of my face were developing with growth and the operations were now being carried out using different techniques to take this growth into consideration. I still could not speak as clearly as I wanted to because of the unusual structure of my palate and the nasal cavities were still out of shape to what they would become. I had to be patient! I was not the most patient of people, as my mum would affirm! Apart from my mum and my sister Betty, everybody else would have difficulty making out what I was trying to say, all I could do was to make gestures to indicate what I wanted to say. You can imagine how I felt when other children spoke to me and I could not express what I wanted to say to them without extreme difficulty, just grunts and gesticulation.

The problems of communication were to get a little worse before they got better, due to the nature of the operations that I was to undergo in order to build up the proper shape of my palate. In this process, I could not answer the other children when they spoke to me. This was a critical time for me! Just when I was beginning to be able to answer back to my friends, this was curtailed when I had to have another operation. You can imagine how frustrated I felt about it, but I had no choice in the matter, it had to be continued until that part of the treatment was completed. I did not look forward to meeting other children when moving up to the various year classes, as I had to start all over again learning to communicate with new classmates. I enjoyed the lessons from a book-reading and writing point of view, because it took my mind off my immediate difficulties. I did get to the stage at one time in just not bothering to talk at all, because it was just too much trouble.

Between operations I could go to school and try to catch up on some of my education, but it proved difficult because of the interruptions along the way. I began facing very unpleasant experiences while at school because of my speech. From the point of view of my fellow classmates, the fact I couldn't speak properly, meant also, that I had something wrong with my brain! As I have said, there wasn't a problem with my brain, at least I didn't think so at the time! But the other children didn't understand this. Underneath all this impediment was a real person trying to get out and prove he was the same as everyone else! This is a reaction which can only be expected from youngsters of that age, and they didn't know any different, unless, of course, they had been taught by their parents how to treat people who were different to themselves, or appear to be different.

As some children get older they become quite unkind and insulting towards others who appear to be timid or look different to everyone else, this usually takes place when a group of youngsters get together to 'have fun' with this or that person for one reason or another. You might say they take on a 'wolf pack' attitude towards any unfortunate target of their having fun activity. There were times that I couldn't face going to school because of this attitude in others in the classroom. At eight or nine, I still couldn't make my self understood, even the teachers did not understand me! It wasn't their fault, it was just one of those things. I didn't appreciate this myself at the time. All I felt was, I was being treated wrongly. My only response to all this was to avoid going to school as much as possible by feigning illness on occasion. My parents would say "You must ignore the comments made by these other children, they will get tired of it before long", but that was easier said than done. They never seemed to get tired of their antics towards me. Loads of advice was being directed towards me, even from friends outside of school, they did not have to cope with the situation.

It was towards the end of 1946 and I still had to go back and forth to hospital for further treatment. The next operation would be to carry out skin grafting to my top lip, which again would prove a painful procedure. As you know, when you eat, the top lip moves around quite a bit, so I had to eat soft food for some time; this was, of course, a very important stage of my treatment as it would result in a big improvement to my profile and general facial appearance. Psychologically it would help me in my lack of confidence in being able to face other people, especially other children, but I didn't appreciate that aspect of the treatment. It was only much later in my treatment that I realised why certain procedures were carried out when they were. When you think about it, there are so many matters to take into consideration in plastic surgery on those so young, what with the natural growth taking place and the allowances for future growth to be made.

By this time I had two younger sisters; Beryl born in 1943 and Vivienne Born in 1946. So we had a full house at home. We still lived in the same place in Tottenham, where all the boys were crammed into one bedroom, the girls in a smaller room and mum and dad in the main bedroom. There was, you can imagine, not much privacy! One thing I always remember was that my oldest sister, Betty, was always there for me. Whenever I was in trouble, she would come to my rescue and speak up for me, because I was unable to express myself clearly, I think on reflection! She acted as my spokesperson. She would come to my defence and encourage me. It was very strange; whenever I had a problem, rather than go to Mum or Dad, I would go to Betty, I knew I could count on her to help! My other brothers and sisters would also help me, if they could, but they were often busy doing other things. Besides! Betty was the one to help me with understanding what I wanted to say.

Betty has passed away some few years ago now, and I still miss her, none-the-less. I didn't have many dealings with my father as he was always busy working with his radio repairs and such. He just didn't have the time to deal with my special needs. Ray, my eldest brother had started work, so this helped a bit with the cost of everything while the rest of us were still at school.

Now, you may have got the impression from what you have read up to now, that I was a poor little innocent boy, who was unfortunate enough to have been born with a number of problems. Well the latter bit was true, but the innocent bit? I can tell you, I was not! I had my moments, and I was a long, long way from perfect, as those who knew me would tell you. I may have been born with facial problems, but the rest of me was normal. I used to play truant from school when I was in the juniors, and once or twice later on. I used to make up the most amazing excuses for my absences on occasion. I used to take money from my mum's purse; not much, but enough to go and have some fun at the fun-fair. I was feeling very sorry for myself and used to try to forget about all my troubles at home and at school. I could not blame my condition for me doing things like this, but I used it as an excuse to myself. I was later to regret very much what I had been doing, because one day I was found out. My dad walked me down to the police station to see the 'nice policeman' for him to have a talk to me about what I was doing. He showed me a 'nice little room with yellow coloured bars' and he said to me, "This will be your new home if you continue to do the things you are doing". I was "visibly shocked" my dad said later. I was never to do anything like this again. I was to learn that when you think that you are missing out on anything, you don't just take it, or steal it!

On the more positive side to my nature though, I loved swimming, although I recall my mother thought I would never be able to swim due to my breathing problems. I just could not breathe through my nose very well. But this turned out to be an advantage because you don't breathe underwater do you? In fact as I grew older, swimming played a very important part in my life.

The first encounter with anyone is with the face and the speech. This cannot be disguised or hidden, unless you wear a mask and you can't go round wearing a mask all the time. As for speech - well! I'll leave that to your imagination. So, anyone who happens to present a less than perfect image, this can be almost any disability, not necessarily facial or speech problems but other physical impairments, can mean several years of difficulty and embarrassment caused by the ignorance and attitude of our peers. It seems at times that anyone who cannot present the so-called 'perfect image', 'as seen on tv', becomes the object of taunting by this particular group of children and young adults. I have to say from my own experience, that not all members of my peer group were willing to join in the 'making fun of' sessions, there were some who would act in a protective manner towards me and try to discourage others from displaying this bad attitude. It was clear that some could display an understanding of the difficulties that people in my position had to cope with.

People do strange things though! I recall a particular instance of one youngster who was about 13 years of age when I was age nine. He was displaying a mocking, threatening and really rude attitude towards me in front of all his friends, who thought it great fun at the time. One of my friends who was with me was trying to stop what was going on, but to no avail. I'm not sure what happened next, but suddenly I let fly and knocked this lad to the ground and left him stunned. Just as suddenly I realised that I may have hurt him and immediately bent down to him saying,

"I was sorry for doing that" at the same time helping him up. It was most unlike me because I was not keen on hitting out on anyone, specially someone bigger than me! Well, the strange upshot of this was, we were to become friends for the rest of our school days. He was to become one who would rise to my aid when other incidents took place, and they did. It took just a bit of 'education' to put a stop to this kind of treatment. To a certain degree, I had to get used to this sort of thing happening on occasion during my school days.

To go back a little, when I was between eight and nine years of age, I was undergoing vital operations that were to make such a big difference to my life in the way I was going to look eventually. I used to lay on my bed in the ward and think about my brothers and sisters and what they were doing, and how they were getting on at school. My brother Ray had started work, and I began to wonder if I would ever be able to get work. For one thing, I had to overcome my difficulty in being able to talk and to express myself. So much depended on how I would look after all this was over. Would I be able to get work, what would I do? One thing for sure, I didn't want to be left behind. I had come through these operations somehow, and this attitude seemed to be building up from within me. I was determined to overcome any difficulties that lay ahead. As for being left behind, this was not going to happen!

From 1948 to 1957 I was going back and forth to hospital for the various operations, sometimes on my own. If anyone asked me to tell them which of the operations I considered to be most vital and significant in my life up to that point in time, I would have said, the operations that took place during the years 1944 to 1946. This was when the procedure being carried out to build up my new palate (roof) was taking place and a bone graft between my nostrils at the front of the nose, which was out of shape from birth (flat), due to the extent of the cleft-palate. Even now the air passages that enable one to breathe through the nasal passages are, for me, still partially blocked, making it difficult to breathe through my nose for any length of time. Operations that took place during 1951-1953 to further improve facial profile and features were also very important for psychological reasons, because I was in the process of preparing to join the wide world of work. Speech-therapy sessions in 1957 to 1959 were very necessary if I was to make any headway at all in the world of work and communication. Whilst going through this process, I didn't fully realise how important this would become until they were nearly completed. I suppose I had developed some 'not very helpful' habits in trying to speak so I felt comfortable in 'just managing' with the situation as it was. I had to unlearn, if that is the correct expression to use, many of the ways I said words. I certainly could not use the letters T,S,C in words in a clear distinctive way, so as to be understood. I probably took it for granted that I could be understood in the way I was speaking. Even my parents and siblings could not understand me once I got into these bad habits. The only true way for me was to write things down; I could just about manage that!

To back-track slightly. I was nearly 10 years of age. My brothers Frank and David were doing fine at school, Frank had only one year more to do at school; then you had to leave at age 15 if you did not go to grammar school. In my case I had lost so many school sessions that I spent all my time trying to catch up with my year group. I had to rely on my own resources, especially when I was in hospital or getting over an operation. This stop-start method of education was not helpful at all! In those days the educational authorities didn't seem to be that bothered about people in my situation, so things just dragged on in a confused and disconnected sort of way, not really achieving very much at all. So, having decided I was not going to be left behind, I realised that if I was to make any progress in my education, then I was the one who was going to do something about it! I was now 10 years of age and I thought to myself, I've only five years left to make any difference to my position when I finally leave school. I used to do a lot of thinking about the future at that stage in my life; it's just as well that I did; nobody was going to do it for me! I had to learn very early in my life that if you want something done, then you had to start the ball rolling. Well, I had so much time on my own following operations, how better to spend the time catching up on everything!

There were times when I wondered whether I could ever reach the stage when I would be able to compete with my peers, as they all seemed to be doing so well, so they used to inform me!

It left me wondering what, if anything, I could do to remedy my situation with my basic education. I used to speak to the teachers about this, but although they said lots of encouraging words, like "I'm sure that you will be fine when the time comes for you to leave school" and "Don't worry, you will be alright" but there was very little practical help that they could offer at the time, largely because of the way the system worked then. Once you left school, you were on your own, that was it! At that time, I still needed one-to-one attention in some areas of education, not because I was unteachable or thick, it was mainly because of the class sizes in those days. There would be as many as 40 or 45 in a class, so you can imagine the teachers' dilemma in trying to reach those who needed special attention, so it wasn't their fault in most cases. The attitude was "If you did not learn, then that was your fault". The system took no prisoners. The teachers' hopes were that the pupils would learn sufficiently to prepare them for the then 11 plus exam when the time came. If you did not pass, then you were sent to the local Secondary Modern School where the teaching staff would do their best to educate and prepare you for work before you left school. Unlike today, there was no sense of achievement at these schools, except on the rare occasion when they were presented with a pupil who showed a spark of ability in any particular area, then they would receive special attention in order to 'bring them on' and maybe allow the pupil to sit another exam to enable he/she to go on to grammar school should they pass, but this was rare. All I can say is, it's a good thing today that we have the system that now operates, where pupils who are 'late developers' can have the opportunity to make progress through the comprehensive system of primary education.

From the age of 10, I found a new source of interest. If anyone wanted to find me, they would have to go along to the local swimming baths. I had learned to swim at a fairly early age, and it proved one area where I could excel! The baths became my 'second home'. I grew to love the freedom that swimming gave me and got quite proficient in all the strokes and in diving, despite my parents' belief that I would never be able to swim and cope with the water etc. I simply had to prove them wrong! I used to go with my brother and his friends and would spend hours in the pool, until the attendants would ask us to "get out" because our time was up to leave the pool. We had many happy times at the baths and it was the place where I was able to build-up my confidence. People in the baths would look at my swimming ability and skills instead of looking at my facial features. This made a big difference to me, they were not trying to understand me when I talked, so the embarrassment was not too acute, I could take my mind off all that for the moment! I was able to gain a few more friends through my swimming activities. My hope was to try to get them to accept me for what I was capable of instead of making fun of me for what I could not do. I felt I could lose myself in the pre- occupation of my swimming and diving, which meant a great deal to me. I could escape into a world of my own, and enjoy the freedom from being looked at as an object of fun by others looking at me for different reasons. I felt good about that! As soon as I got out of the swimming pool I found myself back to the 'old life' again.

At age 11 to 12 I started to think about my lack of ability to communicate with others, especially my friends and relatives. I started to work really hard on my speaking so as to make sense in the face of others and to enable them to understand what I was trying to say. I still had trouble with some of my peers, as I said before, but you get this everywhere you go, particularly if they notice any difference about you compared with others. With me, they couldn't fail to notice these differences, they were only too obvious! It would not be until I was 17 or more before I was to make any significant progress in my speaking. This was yet a long way off and I had a lot of work to do before then. As I grew older into my teens, I become more and more conscious of the fact of my lack of communication skills. I desperately wanted to be able to speak in such a way so as to allow my listeners to understand what I was saying. It was something of an acute embarrassment to me. I went through a stage of not speaking to anyone if I could possibly avoid it. My relatives tried to encourage me by saying "the more I spoke, the better and easier it would become". I thought, well, they were not in my position, so how could they know how difficult it would be for me?

I must mention again my experience at the Mission hall that I attended. I had been attending this place since I was around the age of seven, when I was able to, and now at the age of 11 or 12, I was still there. I remember one particular leader by the name of Gwynn Griffiths who was like a father figure to me. He had great patience with me, and he needed it! He helped me a great deal and I'm sure he didn't realise to what extent that help would mean to me. He would teach me patience in the face of extreme difficulty. This help was to have a practical application, as well as to create in me a trust in God for any help I needed in order to make progress in my speaking and communication generally. At this time I didn't know what to believe about God or Jesus and such but I always felt that there was something more to life than simply this existence. I used to think about these things in my quieter moments. Gwynn was one of the people who had a great influence on my life at that time, when so many changes were taking place in my appearance and experience. All of us in the Covenanter's (a national youth organisation in the missions and churches throughout England) class of 1948-55 found Gwynn to be a most generous and patient person. When I look back on the days, I cannot thank God enough for such a person as Gwynn. He made a real difference in my life. He made some unbearable experiences, bearable! By the time I was 15, I had experienced three years of happiness and relative contentment at the Mission, and I just mention here (in case they ever read this account), so as to acknowledge my thanks to them for their friendship and support at a time in my life when that friendship was vital. Nicky, Dave, Richard, Julia, Colin and many more, you know who you are! Thank you for what you were to me. The Mission, like the swimming baths, were a kind of haven to me. At one place I could count on the friendship of my classmates and at the other I could concentrate on my swimming activities and excel in the things I could really do. To the leaders of the group at the Mission, I say thank you for making a big difference in my life.

At 14 I joined the senior group of Covenanter's and found being in this group very helpful to me because they seemed to have a lot of patience with me. I was still having trouble making myself understood. I shall always be grateful for the help that the leaders gave me. At this time in my life, I was getting a little more concerned about what I might be doing when I had left school. I was getting ready to leave school at age 15. I had no plans to stay on, as much as I wished to. I had only one year in which I had to make a difference in my educational achievement or any progress that I could make, if any!

You could say, panic stations were the order of the day! My parents, bless them, were not too hopeful about my prospects, and perhaps understandably so.

In the next chapter I will attempt to explain how I coped with the massive turning point in my struggles to find work and communicate with the outside world of work experience. Would I or wouldn't I make a go of it?

Chapter 3

Turning Point

It was a difficult and testing time as I struggled to cope with a steep learning curve, with trying to speak clearly and catching up with my school work as I had lost so much because of the operations.

There were times when I observed my friends at the Mission in what they were saying about how they were getting on at school in their exams. Of course I remained quiet. It struck me that unless I made a determined effort to improve myself I would be left behind. I considered I was just as capable of making progress as they were, but for obvious reasons I had slipped back in my education, as I said before. I thought to myself "It is not too late". I was still only a young man at 14, but I had a lot of catching up to do so I got down to some serious work at school. By the time I was 15 though, I didn't have any qualifications so I had to leave school.

During the year before I left school, I was concerned as to what kind of work I would be able to do. My parents took the view that I would never really be able to get the kind of job that promised a possibility of promotion. They didn't seem to have very much hope for me. I suppose, on a human level, and standing in their shoes, I might have come to the same conclusion. So I don't blame them for the position they held. With the benefit of hindsight, they, like myself, were not taking into consideration what God is able to do. Yes, there were missed opportunities at school but my parents were of the opinion that no matter how much I tried, I would not be able to hold down a job that would give me work satisfaction. They felt it would all be too much for me. When I considered what my brothers and sisters were able to do, I felt, if I was not careful I would be left behind. As I said before this was something I was trying to avoid. So I made a conscious decision to apply for evening classes once I had left school. In the meantime, I would get any kind of work that I could which would enable me to earn a little money whilst building up my missed education. This was to prove a very important decision and make a great deal of difference to my prospects, and would take time and patience would be needed.

The time came at last when I reached 15 and I would have to say goodbye to school. This was to prove the turning point of my life! Paramount in my mind was the fact I could not speak clearly, so you can imagine my thoughts as I prepared to go for interviews for jobs, even for the most menial type of work. It wasn't that I couldn't do more interesting tasks, but merely because those considering taking me on mistakenly thought I was backward because of the way I looked and spoke. I can understand why they would have taken this view. So it was vital that my speech had to be improved as a matter of priority. I began to teach myself to speak. This proved to be an arduous task because I had got into bad habits in the way I would express myself, but this had to stop! With my elder sister helping me, and sometimes my mother helping as well, together with my friends at the Mission, who were also very helpful, it was going to make a difficult task a little easier. I had to work hard though. I did this for about three or four years.

I had said goodbye to school with some trepidation as to what I was going to do for a living. My parents didn't have much to say about this, largely because they didn't know how to advise me about the sort of work I might be able to acquire. I didn't know myself! I visited the local Labour Exchange for some ideas and they didn't know quite what to say to me, and along with others, they thought I was a bit slow in the head as well as not looking the part. Well anyway, this was the impression I got in my conversations with them. I started going around most of the factories in the area looking for the notice boards stating 'vacancies'. In those days there were plenty of jobs on offer for those willing to work. I was 'willing', they couldn't fault me on that! But just how successful I was going to be in finding someone to take me on, was something I had to find out. I must admit to presenting something of a challenge to any would-be-employer. Eventually I found work in a shoe factory, not very far from my home. It was sticking soles on the base of shoes; but I found it all very tedious, a bit 'soul-destroying' really. I did manage the tasks that were required of me and the Manager was quite happy with my work, although I didn't talk very much to him or my work-mates. I stayed there about nine months and then I started looking for more interesting work that would pay a little more each week. I also thought by then that if I was able to get another job, as the manager was happy with my work, he would give me a good reference.

Again I searched for my next job on my own. I avoided the Labour Exchange, for the reasons already given and eventually found a job with a company that made duplicators, amongst other things. During the next four years I found other jobs such as steel furniture making, case making and working for a bakery in their delivery section. Through all this time I was still learning to speak more clearly. I did have to learn to speak three times due to the alterations to the structure of the palate following operations during 1948 and 1954 to1957. So I was still having operations that took me away from my jobs from time to time. This didn't help in keeping down some of the jobs I had because employers were not always that understanding and wouldn't necessarily keep my job open while I was in hospital. Today, of course, this is different. I used to think about the kind of work I would like to do in the future, and it became clear to me that if I was to make any kind of progress in the type of work I could apply for, then I had to make significant progress in my speaking ability. At times I felt very anxious about the progress, or lack of it, that I was making. However, I plodded on in the hope that it would all come together eventually.

All the while this changing of jobs was going on, I had to get used to speaking to my work-mates and other people to do with work along the way. This proved very taxing, right from the day I left school. How glad I was though to have connections with the Mission! When on occasions I began to flounder and get a bit of self-pity going because of apparent lack of progress I was making, my friends there would tell me off, in the 'nicest possible way' and I deserved it! Through their continuous care and concern for me, they would try to encourage me. They were a great source of inspiration to me. I needed the discipline to keep going. Through my association with those at the Mission, I gradually came to the conclusion that I wanted whatever made these friends tick.

There was something about them that stood out in stark contrast to the people I worked with or my other friends, or indeed my own family, none of whom at the time were Christians. Although I could not sit in judgement because I too had very unChristian traits! But I knew there was a difficult atmosphere in the home as compared with that of the Mission hall or wherever I met my Christian friends. Then, at age 16, something happened which proved to be an even more important turning point in my life than leaving school.

I had the opportunity to attend a crusade at the Haringey, North London Arena. This was held under the auspices of the Billy Graham Organisation. It was there, in 1954 after attending for three evenings in a row, that I was drawn to the inscription above where Dr Graham was speaking, it read: Jesus said:

'I am the way, the truth, and the life, no one comes to the Father, except by Me' (John 14:6)

It was through these words that I became a Christian. I knew I could no longer rely on my own strength and determination to get me through the challenges that I would face in the future. I began to realise that God had had His hand on my life ever since I was born, and through that I had survived the trauma of the earlier years. Then as I began reading through the Bible, God gave me a promise. This promise came from what God had said to Moses in Exodus 4:11, after he made all sorts of excuses for not speaking to Pharaoh about 'letting his people go', Moses' main excuse being that he 'wasn't eloquent in speech. God's reply to him was "Who gives man your mouth?' These words really hit me and that is why I have called my story "The words of my mouth"! Moses had no answer for this statement and he knew there was no option but to go and speak to Pharaoh as the Lord directed. I figured, if God could enable Moses to speak to the King of Egypt as he eventually did, then the same God would be able to help me! At that point I decided, perhaps naively, if God would enable me to speak, then I would speak for Him. Naivety or not, the Lord knew all about me.

If I was willing to serve Him, then He would give me the ability and equip me for service.

You may wonder why I have included the paragraph above! I could not in all honesty tell my story and give you the impression that I was able to cope on my own. I make no apology for stating the source of the help I received along the way. If what I have shared with you to this point has been any help to you in your life, then I thank God, because my quest is not only to help and encourage those of you who have suffered any disability or are still suffering so, whether physical, spiritual or mental, but also to point you to the One who can help. I believe God has the answer to all your needs as indeed He has met all mine and continues to do so. These needs have not always been met in the way I had anticipated. I have learned to cope in spite of my difficulties and through all these experiences one is in a better position to empathise with those who were and are still struggling to come to terms with their problems.

There is no doubt that attending the Mission in those early years has proved a deciding factor in my appreciation of the help that came from my friends there, young and old alike. These people did not go round saying they were Christians, but they demonstrated it by the way they conducted their lives. It was a case of 'actions speaking louder that words'. The confidence gained in my sharing the good times, as well as the bad times, was to stand me in good stead, and sometimes I did have times when I was full of doubts, I would express my lack of faith on occasion because of the tremendous challenges to my sense of well-being. 'Here was I', so I would think to myself, 'trying to get to grips with my life and be able to rise above all these difficulties strewn in my way, only to be faced with more obstacles'. Looking back on them now, I can see why they were put there! I found that every obstacle I was able to surmount made me that much more determined and stronger. So they were a blessing, not a curse! Although I didn't see it that way at the time.

By this time I had started to attend speech-therapy classes and although they said I made such good progress myself and with the help of others, this was all very much to my surprise and proved very helpful when the therapist got to work on me. Without that my sessions would have had to go on for a much longer period. As it was I spent about a year going through this exercise.

Talking about being confident, there is little doubt that my confidence grew through my swimming activities. With one of my brothers we had started a small swimming club where we taught all ages from five upwards to swim. We also taught diving. The adults proved to be the hardest to teach, mainly because they were carrying a lot of 'baggage', awareness of how one can do harm to themselves if they were not careful, especially when diving. Once they got over these fears then they were fine. For the youngsters, with very few exceptions, they would take all this in their stride.

All this was teaching me lessons on how to overcome difficulties by facing up to them and not letting them get the better of me. The more experience you get in anything you do, the more confident you become. The youngsters' confidence was in the teacher; the adults' confidence had to be nurtured in the face of their age and/or lack of experience or indeed adverse experiences. You might have thought this would be the other way round! But is doesn't work that way. The older you get, the more fearful of the unknown and potential problems or danger you become.

My brother and I received much satisfaction from seeing someone progress from being a fearful non-swimmer to becoming a good swimmer and diver, full of confidence. It was very interesting to see how people coped with and overcame their fears and doubts, then began to gain confidence in their achievements gained through teaching and instruction in the various skills. I have related all this experience of gaining confidence in the area of my own case of learning to communicate with others. There's an old saying: 'Never ask someone to do something that you yourself have not done already'. By obeying this simple rule you can earn the respect of people as they listen to you. If you are going to counsel people, it's better to do so from your own experience – 'I have been there, and have got the tee-shirt!'

I am reminded from scripture that the great Apostle Paul could only share with the Church that which he had already received (1Cor 11:23ff). What if he hadn't received from the Lord, would his preaching have been so effective? I leave the answer to you.

Being able to overcome the difficulties and barriers that are presented to us in life, to be able to scale the mountains of uncertainty and traverse the plain of trial and testing is surely the hope of us all. Truly this is a wonderful and satisfying experience. In a way, this is what this book is about! Finding the strength to be able to overcome the difficulties that one experiences in life's way, whether they are physical, mental, psychological, environmental or even spiritual, there is always a way to find the answer! If the answer is not within you, it may be provided by others, from friends, acquaintances, counsellors, ministers, relatives or the church. Never give up! There are answers! See Philippians 4:12-13 --is this your experience? Look it up!

In the next chapter, I will explain how I had to face up to quite difficult challenges as I was entering my late teens and twenties. What with finding work that would be satisfying and trying to prove that I was just as capable as the next person of holding down a job.

Chapter 4

Teens and Twenties Challenge

By now I was getting on for 19 years of age. My speech was gradually improving, and I found myself being engaged in activities that I would not have been able to do two years earlier - like going round the doors where I lived conducting surveys about how many people within the households attended church. I did this with a friend that I got to know at the Mission hall. This was quite a challenge, as I had not done this type of thing before, and I wasn't sure how I would come over to the people I met. Remember, I did ask God to teach me to speak for Him, and this was my first test to see if it was possible. My friend Ray helped me a great deal during those visits to our neighbourhood. I think God was helping him to help me! I remember how we used to walk everywhere, sometimes from where I used to live in Tottenham right into the City. It was good to walk, the only problem was that Ray was much taller than me and in consequence I had to take two steps to his one. Well, at least I got twice as much exercise in the process!

It was during the years between my 16th and 21st birthdays that I concentrated on trying to catch up on my educational shortfall. This worked reasonably well as I studied Maths, English and Technical Drawing. I thought that if I could make good progress in these areas, then I would be able to make attempts to secure a better and more worthwhile position. The jobs were out there, but would I be able to persuade any prospective employer to accept me? I made up my mind that any future job would involve communicating with my colleagues in the work place and with others in the general way of things. Up to this time I had only been working in a situation where all I had to do was carry out a task according to instructions given without the necessity of talking to anyone, so I was safe! I couldn't remain 'safe' forever, could I? Lots of the tasks that I had to perform were in the area of machine minding or assembling. My heart's desire was to get a job that would give me 'job satisfaction' and the sort of work that I was doing, just didn't achieve this.

I decided that when I had finished my studies, I would try for a different kind of job. Where was I to start? In the end, I thought that I would start in a relatively simple way in order to give me time to get used to the possible demands that I would be faced with in an office of some kind. My parents thought I was aiming a bit high to begin with. I had to convince them that I could do it, and let them see that my faith would carry me through to achieving. This is when my faith would be tested and I would have to make the first step, nobody was going to do it for me.
'God helps those who help themselves.'

I saw advertised a job as a despatch clerk, this entailed writing down details, liaison between carriers, the post-office and other members of the staff. It would be down to me to make a success of this job, but first I had to get through the interview. There were, as it turned out a good number of applicants for the job, so I began to have doubts about my chances of being hired. It finally came for my turn to be interviewed. The questions came thick and fast, at the same time, when answering, I had to be careful to speak as clearly as possible. There were moments when I felt my speech left something to be desired but I pressed on, giving as much information about myself as I could. I left them with the impression that I, despite all the difficulties that I had experienced, was determined to overcome these problems and do a good job. They said "Thank you Mr Chering we will let you know in a few days one way or another". A few days later, much to my surprise and delight, I had been offered the post. My surprise was born out of my lack of faith. But God is faithful. This was an important step for me; the fact that I got this job, would lead to other jobs in the future being offered. Once one is given the opportunity of gaining experience, then it makes matters much easier to deal with later on when required. The job I obtained then seemed so insignificant compared with positions I would hold later in life, but it was such an important first step. My experience with this job would affect the way I would view future opportunities that came my way.

My parents were taken by surprise when I told them about the job, and of course, they were pleased for me. My mum would tell the neighbours that "My son Mike has got a job as a clerk!" This was to them, a really big step, they couldn't believe it at first. To be honest, I couldn't either. I still had a lot to learn about trusting God in all these things. Many things would happen during my life which would be hard to explain to the onlooker, and it would be very difficult to understand what it was that was motivating me. I grew to know within myself, that there was something leading me on in situations that, in the normal course of events, would have compelled me to give in to my limitations, that 'something' was the hand of God on my life. There can be no other explanation!

As time went on, I began to wonder if I would ever get a girl-friend. I used to say to myself, "Why on earth would a girl want to go out with me? Would she be prepared to take me on, with all my baggage and all?" There were so many questions going through my mind at the time, so for the moment I dismissed the thoughts as rather fanciful! I mean, all my friends were gradually getting girl-friends and talking about future marriage! This is another area in my life where I didn't want to get left behind. Again, my parents and siblings were very doubtful if I would ever find anyone who would take me on, even just to go out with, let alone when it came to marriage! Of course, this meant I would gradually lose the company of my friends as they in turn would find themselves a girl-friend. I could hardly still go around with them could I?

I began to feel a little like a gooseberry amidst such company and naturally I started declining invites where I thought I might be in the way. This, of course, happens to everyone in this position. So in the main, I started to go round on my own and occasionally with a friend. I just had to keep hoping that one day I might meet someone who would be interested in going out with me. I always thought, though, that my looks and the way I spoke were against this happening. I remember that my parents would say, just to give me some hope or encouragement in the matter, "Oh you will find someone one day Mike". Deep down they probably did not believe it! I would just have to chew on that for the time being. I thought, "If God meant me to get married some day, then He would send the right person to me". Very often when we are amidst a problem, we cannot see the answer that is right in front of us. Why do I say that? I had forgotten about a girl whom I'd met through the Mission. I was so busy looking in a different direction and feeling sorry for myself, that I couldn't see the answer God had already prepared for me, right in front of my eyes! But I didn't realise this at the time. In the end, I just had to trust God in the matter. Around this time I was working in another small Mission in their Sunday school, where I was helped by a few others, and on occasion a girl called Sylvia. Now Sylvia was one of the Girl Covenanters at the Mission we both attended in Tottenham. The small Mission where we ran the Sunday school was in Wood-Green. When I look back to those days, I'm amazed at the turn of events that brought Sylvia and myself together. Generally people didn't put any significance to my association with Sylvia, we were just working together in the work at this Mission in Wood-Green and were also involved with the young people at the Tottenham Mission. But God saw the situation differently for which I am eternally grateful to Him. I first met Sylvia when I was in the Covenanter groups at about the age of 17 as I have said. Sylvia would have been nearly 16 then. We had worked together off and on within the different Missions and had got to know each other, but it was nothing more than that. After about four years, when I was 21, I began to realise that I was drawn to Sylvia and hoped to go out with her. I liked her a lot, in fact I grew to love her, she was very quiet at the time, and

I kept my thoughts of her to myself for the moment. By the time Sylvia was about 20, she decided to give up her job working for an Assurance Society and go into nursing training. I eventually got up enough courage to ask her out and perhaps go out on a regular basis. By this time my speech was improving, but I still had some work to do on it. So it was that we began to go everywhere together. I count it a great privilege to have met Sylvia; I think she has been a great stabilising influence in my life. I said she was a quiet person; well, I'm glad to say, she is not so now, in the best possible way. There she was, right under my nose all the time whilst I was worrying about whether I would ever get married! I'm sure God has a sense of humour.

The world can be a hard place at times, especially for those who suffer from any disabilities, let alone the more obvious facial imperfections giving rise to difficulties in speaking and communication generally. I suppose the world at large is still learning the lesson of how to treat people in this situation. For sure, you can't judge by appearances and we should not. I am always impressed by people who have overcome the challenges that life has presented to them, and to some, it is an ongoing experience. With help and understanding, patience and tolerance this makes all the difference to many people in this position. If you are one of those fortunate enough to present to the world a perfect example of the human body with no imperfections, this does not mean to say that everything is fine and rosy in your life. There are many who carry imperfections that are not seen with the naked eye, but underneath there is often great turmoil and dissatisfaction of life and often the feeling of vulnerability.

Some would be reluctant to seek help because they do not want to admit the need of help. I suppose you could say "we all have a weak spot" this is true! So what am I saying in this paragraph? From whatever position you are, as the reader of this article, there is help out there! Avail yourself of it and you will surprise yourself about the results that will follow. There are many folk that have considerable difficulties, but somehow they continue to make an impact on society by using the talents they have naturally. Others, if given the opportunity to excel, would also make quite an impact on those around them. Let's not think, when we see someone who has a difficulty in walking, or speaking and is incapacitated in other ways, that that person has nothing to offer; they may very well have more to offer than a person considered more able would. So we must be careful not to judge by appearances!

My next challenge was to be able to use the telephone without the fear of not being understood. It is hard for anyone who does not normally have difficulty in speaking over the phone, to understand where I'm coming from! At the early stages of the operations that became necessary for someone in my position it was inevitable that I would encounter difficulties in this area of development. When one talks to anyone directly 'face to face' you can at least indicate by gesture if you are having difficulties in being understood, but over the phone; this gave me more problems than quite a lot of others that I was experiencing at the time. It certainly was a challenge! I remember at one time working for a company when part of my duties was to answer the phone and take down the messages that were given for the respective departments. I was called at the time 'duty clerk'. Had I realised what I was taking on as part of the job, I wouldn't have accepted the position. I could do everything else that was required of me, but the telephone! Unfortunately, I had to leave that employment, until such time I was ready to be able to speak with confidence over the phone. Although my speech by this time had improved, but not to the extent I required, or that was required of me. At 18 years of age, I came to realise I had a hill to climb as far as my communication skills were concerned. Not everything was lost though, indeed I felt that I could learn from the experience and it made me all the more determined to overcome this difficulty by perseverance and patience. Up to this point in my work experience, I had only worked in situations that did not require me to speak to my working colleagues to any great extent. I would have to listen very carefully to any instructions given and carry out the task, which I did with no problem at all. In a way, I was glad at this time to remain 'in the background', where I felt safe and out of sight. I must say, that this attitude of mine was not conducive to getting to grips with my learning curve as far as speaking was concerned. When thinking of those days, I felt that I displayed a distinct lack of faith in the light of what I had committed myself to do and to be; 'to speak up and trust God'. I knew deep down that He would enable me to speak in a way that I could be understood, but on occasions, I forgot this! Occasionally I would, in my mind, hold a 'pity party' doubting, feeling sorry for myself, uncertainty, forgetfulness, lack of a positive ego, lack of vision for the future, all the things that go for stunting one's growth and maturity would set in. Then I would have a mood swing in the opposite direction.

This learning curve was becoming more and more

acute, because I wanted to get on in life. I could observe others making progress in their lives, but for me, I felt on occasion, that I was going backwards. How was it to become possible for me to make the progress I desperately sought? On occasion, my impatience would get the better of me. I would be told by my friends that I should seek to make haste slowly. Often my reactions would be, "Well! It's alright for them, they haven't got my problems". I did, in the end, come to realise that it was my own fault. I tell you this so that you will realise, I was a normal person inside trying to get out, I wasn't perfect, far from it! Like everyone else, I had to learn. I spoke to my friends and acquaintances about the problem, and basically they came to the same conclusion as me. Nobody would be able to secure the type of employment that I sought for me, I had to do that myself.

These difficulties I have shared with you are just a few examples of those I had to face during this time in my life. I was seeking, psychologically and in reality, to be accepted by my peers, and all the people I knew. Still the biggest challenge of them all, when I became a Christian, was to be able to tell people what had happened to me. At the risk of losing some of my friends and falling out of favour with others along the way. This, of course, I accepted as part of the cost of discipleship. Many of my non-church friends would say "I was using my church/faith experience as a crutch", but this was not true and still is untrue. I had to work extremely hard to overcome my speaking problems, no-one could do this for me! I had to do it for myself, as I have already said.

There's an old saying, forgive me if I repeat it here:

"God helps those who help themselves". This applies to everyone in one way or another, but particularly for me at this stage of my life. At the end of the day, my friends had to decide whether I was genuine or not. Quite a few of them were surprised at my progress, for they knew what struggles I had had in the past, and were pleased for me, at the same time encouraging towards me by the way they treated me. Others just went their way, not quite knowing what to do or say to me. I must say though, I made many more friends through my experiences and I still am in touch with some in these days 60 years later. I met many friends who were to become through my association with the various churches and groups, like extensions to my family.

I share with you some of my experiences in the hope they might be of some help and encouragement to people who are finding life a difficult journey. I believe we can overcome many of our problems if 'we keep on, keeping on'. Just when at certain times we feel like throwing in the towel, we can say to ourselves, 'Why should I?' Let's re-light the spark within us and let's reject all within us that would pull us down to the sorry depths of despair and self-pity. We can rise above these problems! The more we resist the one who would pull us down, the stronger we become. I have found this to be my experience, and still do! Is it yours?

At times in my life I would have found it to be easy to just give up the struggle in trying to communicate with others rather than face the obvious difficulties when it came to meeting with people generally and speaking to them. There have been those moments when everything seemed to go wrong, then I would ask myself 'What's the point of it all?' Often I would go into this kind of thinking, as I have stated before, it can become all very negative. I suppose, on a human level, it was the result of many setbacks in any progress I was making. Very frustrating! Somehow, I had to try and get myself out of this frame of mind and eventually ask myself, 'What purpose would it serve to give up now?' At the end of the day, it is always better to have made an attempt and fall a little short, than not bother at all and achieve absolutely nothing! The measure of satisfaction derived from perseverance in the face of difficulty, was well worth it. I couldn't, and wouldn't, let myself become smug though, otherwise I would be brought down to earth with a jolt.

There is a sense of pride that one can have and should have in one's achievements. This applies to everyone. Sometimes the odds stacked against you are tremendously harsh, whether you are up against disabilities of any nature or problems with ethnicity, or indeed social standing. In our better moments, we can have the positive thought, 'I can be as good as the next person'.

I've explained before about my swimming activities and I believe it was through this experience that I gained more confidence in being able to communicate with others. At the time, it was not so much the speaking itself, because that was far from perfect, but it was the ability to communicate to people in general what I wanted them to know. As I observed the confidence being built up in those I was teaching about swimming, so it would be a real encouragement to myself, and I found this to be a rewarding experience. Instead of gesticulating with my hands all the time, I was beginning to say what I wanted them to understand, even though I had some way to go before I would be able to speak with confidence. I knew this would take time to achieve. All these activities helped me to overcome my reticence to share with others verbally. It's all very catching when one observes somebody doing something successfully and one thinks 'I can do that!' When I look back to those times, I remember that the experiences I had in being involved with people generally, gave me the opportunity to build up my speaking ability both with family and friends.

While all this activity was going on, I was attending a youth class at the Mission I mentioned before. I longed for the time that I would be able to take part in the discussions that took place. I would just sit there, wondering if I should try to say something, very often I would chicken out, being afraid to make myself look silly, or not be able to actually say what I wanted. I was still learning how to express myself verbally, and it was difficult! The more I thought about it, the worse it became for me to say anything. When someone would ask me a question, I would have to think very carefully as to how I was to give the answer, at that time it didn't come naturally. It still doesn't come naturally even at my age. I still have to consider how I am to speak, but, of course, it has become somewhat easier over the years. For someone who is unaffected by speaking problems, immediate answering is no problem, you take it for granted!

It is amazing how God works! He knew I needed to be able to speak clearly and with considerable thought so as to make myself understood clearly. I believe it was all the various circumstances that came my way, through having to speak to my friends, family, working colleagues and other contacts, that gave me the training that I needed in order to face the world of communication. I never set out to learn these lessons in this way. I could have ignored these opportunities and turned away through fear of embarrassment because I didn't want to make a fool of myself in front of others. With the benefit of hindsight, as I look back on those times, I realise that God knew what was ahead in my life, and He was equipping me, although I had no idea what would become of me later in life.

I think back to the time when I was age 16. The first challenge I faced was when one of the teachers at the Mission talked to me about baptism. I had become a Christian about three months earlier. It was the custom at that time (and still is within Baptist churches) to say how you became a Christian. Now, up to that point in time, I had never spoken in public and the idea of speaking in front of a large crowd of people became a major concern in my mind. It frightened the life out of me! But then I eventually plucked up enough courage to enquire further about baptismal classes. The person who spoke to me about baptism in the first place was very supportive and encouraged me to go forward in faith. I thought at the time 'It's easy for him to say that'. Nevertheless I did take that step and started to attend the classes, for a short course on what it means to be a Christian and go through the waters of baptism. The Minister at the local Baptist church ran the course. He had a way with words to the degree that you could not fail to understand what he was talking about.

The day came at last for the baptismal service to be held. I was 'shaking in my boots' for want of a better expression! But I did manage to speak. I was certainly glad when that was all over, not the baptism, but the speaking bit. Some very kindly folk came up to me and said, 'You spoke very well and clearly, you wouldn't have known that you had all those operations'. I'm sure this was out of kindness in order to encourage me, but it was nice of them. I was later to find out that I had actually come over quite clearly and they were not just being nice!

Chapter 5

The Real World of Communication

I shall never forget that first occasion to speak at my baptism at the age of 16, it was to mark a real turning point in my life when I was in my late teens, 18 to 19 years old. It was decided, after years of operations that involved plastic surgery and the like, including skin grafting, that they would now concentrate on the dental side of the treatment. My teeth, in what was supposed to be the roof and gums of my mouth, were up to this point all out of place, this was the result of severe clefting of my palate at birth. The plan now was to remove all these displaced teeth and create a mould by which they would be able to take impressions for a special plate to be inserted in where the roof of my mouth should be. This would ensure the true alignment of the top teeth with the lower teeth, which were ok. I had to wait for this process to begin and join the queue like everyone else. This treatment would take some considerable time to achieve its completion, and in the meantime I would lose any progress that I had made in my elocution, but the end result would be worthwhile waiting for. This, of course, was at a critical time in my life as I was seeking to find more suitable work and be able to communicate better with my friends and others.

I had a number of questions about this stage of the treatment: I wanted to know how long it would take; would I lose all the progress I had made over the years in learning to speak to the degree I had reached; how was I going to manage with employment issues, bearing in mind, I was having more contact with people in my work experience; and how long would it take for me to acquire the necessary skills in order to communicate with others again? These questions were swimming around in my mind as time went on. I needn't have worried about this, but at the time I didn't realise this - I am a bit of a worrier as my wife will tell you! Hindsight is a wonderful thing is it not? If only we could see ahead, but we can't, and do you know what? On reflection, I'm glad this is the case.

This dental treatment started in mid 1957 and went on well into 1958 before it was finally completed. It involved going back and forth to the hospital every five or six weeks for a few days at a time. This was because the treatment involved taking out a series of teeth which were growing in the wrong place, and they had to be careful not to affect the places where they had already operated on when building the palate. So it took time. This procedure obviously interrupted my working pattern with the employer at the time, and fortunately they were very good in keeping my position open for me. As I was working for a duplicator manufacturer, I did not need to do too much talking in the process of doing my job. When I think about it, it was the right time for me to have that treatment. I think if I had been working for another employer, it may not have turned out so convenient for everyone.

I was, of course, concerned that I couldn't speak to all

my friends at this time, but they were brilliant in the way they helped me. Once the treatment was over I had to start learning to speak all over again, because the structure of my mouth had altered drastically. When the new plate was finally fitted, it felt as though I had a mouth full of china! It was a while before I got used to it, I couldn't eat or talk properly.

Eventually I did get used to this new 'plate of china' (my teeth!) whereas before, when I talked, I couldn't pronounce certain consonant sounds like 'S' or 'T' but when I got used to this situation with my new plate, I began to be able to utter for the first time these consonant sounds. It was a steep learning curve, but I was glad to be able to negotiate these sounds, and in time it proved that this treatment was to be really worthwhile and an important turning point in my communication with others. Altogether it took about a year to get my speech back to what it was, but with a vital difference: I was able to speak a lot clearer. Everyone I met after going through this treatment remarked how much more of a improvement there was in my speech and my looks (profile). I was so relieved about this and it gave me greater confidence in meeting people.

Before all this took place, I was always keen on sharing what God had done for me in my speaking for Him. After the treatment I remembered what I felt at the time I became a Christian, that if God helped me to speak, then I would speak for Him. I remembered what He said to Moses (Exod 4:11) , so I thought, "Well! if He helped Moses, then He can help me!" God is faithful in His promises. I'm only an ordinary chap, but God is extraordinary in all His dealings with us. I will be forever grateful for all the help that I received in my younger days by so many people of all ages. When we need help in any area of our lives, then we must work in co-operation with others who are trying to help us. The same goes for help we receive from God;- He needs our co-operation too! I could have sat back and waited for a miracle of speech to happen, but it doesn't happen that way as a general rule. We cannot 'put God in a matchbox'. God is able to do exceedingly, abundantly above all we think or ask, often it is through ourselves that things begin to happen which we think are not possible. We are often the hands, feet, legs, heart and minds that He needs to establish His perfect will.

Then came another challenge! You will recall, I said I had to work in factory situations because I had no qualifications and could not make myself clearly understood. Well, by the time I was nearly twenty, I began getting very unsettled in what I was doing work-wise. Remember, it was at this time I was undergoing dental treatment which was going to make all the difference to my speaking ability, but it would all take time. I knew I had to have patience in all this, dental treatment was not my idea of having fun! I was facing having about 22 teeth out from the area surrounding the palate.

You can't imagine how relieved I was when this phase of my treatment was over. Perhaps now, I could start to live my life in the normal way. I thought to myself I would be able to answer the phone, speak much better and feel more confident when speaking to strangers, without having to use other methods of communication; give answers to questions put to me without having unseemly long delays before answering in my quests to formulate the words in my mouth; this meant a great deal to me! I could even contemplate getting a better type of occupation. Needless to say, I was looking forward to 'getting out there' and making my mark, at last! After all the years of waiting and struggling to make myself understood, there presented for me the opportunity to venture out into 'the real world of communication'. I felt I had to seize the moment to make some kind of impression in order to let people know that I could be 'as good as the next person'; only time would tell!

As mentioned before, I managed to get a job as a despatch clerk. It was better than working in a factory; not that there is anything wrong in working in a factory, it depends what you want to do in life, but for me, I needed to be challenged in so far as my speech was concerned. Even when I was younger, I was happy with figures and writing etc but this job presented the opportunity to converse with others in the office and other members of the staff, as well as people from other companies in the course of the work. Now I knew it was only by placing myself in these sorts of situations that I would have to develop the type of skills that were required, if I was to make progress in my communicating abilities. At this time I was still attending evening classes in my efforts to catch-up on missed education. This was beginning to be very vital and necessary if I was to secure better employment later on. I had started night school after I left school at 15, I was so glad I had the foresight to do this, because had I left it until the time I had finished my treatment, it may had been too late. I carried on in this job for a while until I gradually began to feel that I could do more interesting work. By this time my dental treatment was over and I was free to pursue my desire to obtain more satisfying and challenging work. Bearing in mind my inbuilt impatience, I was quite restless and eager to move on to getting more experience, so I decided to look around for other jobs as and when they came up. In those days one could virtually walk out of one job into another, but of course, it depended on what you were looking for! After some while I saw a job advertised asking for a sales clerk in a trading office in London. It was a cable company, selling anything to do with cable fittings and cable itself. In this case, I had the further opportunity to develop my speaking abilities with both staff and customers. It promised to be quite interesting work. I must have made some kind of impression, because I was taken on. I found the work interesting to a degree.

I decided to stick at it for a while, it was all good experience and would be good for future references should I need them. I had to practise my speaking quite a lot, because in my case, I needed to manipulate my tongue three times as much to be able to pronounce and enunciate my words in order to make them sound the same as when others speak. Even now I have to think about how I am going to say something, but I get there in the end!

There were other areas of interest I had where speaking was to become very important to me. I was keen on helping in the Sunday school classes and the youth clubs, I spoke about earlier. Although I was helping in a general way, I did aspire to be able to take a class and help in the speaking to the youngsters and others. I knew what I wanted to say, but the difficulty was to be able to actually say it! This was a challenge to me which I had to rise to.

Now, if anyone had told me when I was 12 that I would one day be engaged in speaking to a group of children or teenagers or even adults, and be able to hold down a job that involved speaking to lots of different people from all walks of life, I simply wouldn't had believed them! Between the ages of 19 and 21 I found myself teaching in the Sunday school and taking part in the leadership of my Covenanter Group. By this time, as I said before, I had finished the dental treatment. I was now on the way to speaking more clearly as I got used to my new situation.

Whilst attending the Mission, I also began helping another church called 'The Welcome Mission'. It certainly lived up to its name! The Sunday school needed some help. Now I wasn't sure how I would be received, because they were all strangers to me, particularly from the point of view of the children. I had met the adults some time before, so this helped. Eventually the numbers grew and I became its superintendent. Later with others including Sylvia (who became one of the young people at our own Mission in Tottenham) and together we ran the group. Many happy days were spent at that church. I have a particular reason for my affection for that place because it was the first place that I was to take an adult service on my own. Why do I say that? Well, at our own Mission we had two teams of young people. Every now and again we would go to another church to take services (all for good experience purposes) and we would take it in turns to conduct the service and take the various parts. This was in order to gain experience in the different aspects of the service and to discover the 'talents' of the various people involved. I had taken part in one of the services, but never had I done the talk. This was the case up to when I took the whole service at the 'Welcome Mission'. I was then 21 years old. I was received very warmly. I must say my knees were knocking together and I'm sure that the congregation could hear them! The next few years were spent there.

These are some of the activities I found myself starting to be engaged in at nearly 21 years of age. Most people who knew me well were very surprised that I was into these areas of interest. Having said all this I knew that there was a long way to go! Some of the people who had known me since the early days thought I should not push myself, they felt that I should be content with the progress I had made up to that point. I can understand where they were coming from and why they felt this way. They knew the problems I had experienced along the way, and they had my best interests at heart, but I was determined to make as much progress as I could, and the only way ahead was to be gained by practise, practise, practise! Let alone 'education, education, education'. I was very aware that God would enable me to achieve the goals I had set in my heart, and that God would help me reach my heart's desire. I only had one answer to those who would question why I was taking so much upon myself. 'I have come this far along a difficult road, why not go further?' On reflection, if I had heeded the advice given to me at that point, no matter how well intentioned, I would have made very little further progress, nor indeed, obtained more interesting employment which I was to procure in future days. Who knows what opportunities I could have missed had I stopped making an effort at that point? It all became a matter of faith and confidence to face the future. These two elements work together! I believe this applies to anyone wishing to overcome difficulties and being able to face up to the challenges that are often presented in our lives.

In April 1959 I had reached 21 years of age. I had been attending night-school for about six years. At this time I felt the urge to take a further step of faith by securing a job that involved speaking directly to the general public. But what was this job to be? The previous jobs I'd had no longer held any challenge for me. Of course, I was thankful for all the different experiences I had acquired since leaving school, but I knew that it could not be the sum total of my life's work experience. There just had to be more, and I was determined to find out what it was!

I made the decision to actively seek work that would give me job satisfaction and contact with the public, but, as I have said, I also knew that this may take time to achieve. At this time I was still working for the cable manufacturer in London and although I quite liked the job and the people I worked with, I realised that this job held no long-term prospects for me. It was secure enough but this was not the only criterion to be considered. I needed an occupation that involved my brain and had a bit of a challenge about it. Once having found the sort of work I was looking for, I would ask myself, would they accept me? Would I fit the bill as far as the employer was concerned? Could I persuade the employer to give me a trial and would my speaking ability be good enough? All these questions were coming into my mind. I was indeed, making reasonable progress in my speaking.

I kept on practising in order to polish up my speaking

in certain areas, just in case! I spoke to my friends and family about my intentions in order to get some form of consensus as to their opinion.

I did find that the most positive encouragement came from my friends and the people I worked with at the Mission, although my siblings were quite helpful, but had some reservations as to how far I could go with this. My parents thought, because of all the troubles I had experienced, I did not have the same level of confidence as others. From their standpoint, it was better if I hung on to the job I was already doing, where I was relatively 'safe' than to take a chance in venturing out into unknown territory with all its difficulties. In a way, I understand why they thought this! But I had to prove to them that I was not alone in my quest and that there was 'someone' helping me. I do feel in hindsight, that they did have my interests at heart. Now, here is the rub, I had to launch out in faith for an occupation that I had hitherto not considered or had any experience of before. God was going to show me that with Him 'all things were possible'. As the Negro-spiritual term has it: "I have seen the promised land, but as yet I have not reached it".

I was still a member of the fellowship at the Mission and was getting experience as one of the leaders of the group of young people. Actually there were two groups, girls and boys between the ages of 15-20. We used to go out from the Mission on occasion to visit other churches in the area. The purpose of these visits was for each member to gain experience in leading, speaking and conducting the services for young people and adults alike, as I have said. You will recall I spoke about Sylvia who came to help at the small Mission hall with the Sunday school, well, she was one of the group of girls at the Mission in Tottenham. You will also recall that I had spent a few years at the small Mission hall in Wood-Green. After I had finished there, I came back to Tottenham to help with the young people there. It was there I met up with Sylvia again. I started to go out on a casual basis with her and the rest of the group. I didn't know it then, but Sylvia was to become my wife on 12th May 1962 when I would have reached the age of 24.

All this experience also acted as the precursor to more involvement in public speaking later in my life, I also didn't realise to what extent at that time. Again, with hindsight, I can see how the Lord was training and enabling me to speak for Him as promised. Things don't just happen by looking at them or wishing them into existence, you have to do something about them! If something is laid on your heart, then it is a good indication, that it is you or I upon which the burden of action may fall. It's no good waiting for someone else to move! They may be moved to act in a different direction.

In August 1960 Sylvia decided to take up nursing and resigned her job working in an insurance office and took up her studies in the then State Enrolled Nursing Course at St Anne's Hospital in Tottenham. It was at about this time that Sylvia and I started to go out together. I had always liked her right from the days she started helping at the Mission in Wood-green, but I had kept my thoughts about her to myself. I was so pleased when she said that we could go out together. There were times I never thought this would happen! It was during the next couple of weeks that Sylvia decided she would be going into nursing training. We discussed this together quite a bit. Then suddenly she had the idea that if she left the insurance society, and this would be soon, perhaps I could apply for her job to replace her. She knew that I wanted to get a more satisfying and challenging job where I would have the opportunity to meet people. My query was could I hold down such a position? This threw me for a little while, but then I began to see that God had a sense of humour. Me! Working for an insurance co? I would have to seriously consider all this. Sylvia told me what may be involved in the job, and the more she told me, the more my ears pricked up as I took on board the implications of being engaged in the work of this nature. It meant talking to clients, agents and staff and would involve lots of telephone work, it was all talking, talking and maths. I was quite happy with the maths side of things, but the constant talking! This was to be quite a challenge. So many questions in my mind, what was I to do? Would I be able to cope? I suppose that after waiting for so long to be able to speak clearly, it was understandable that I should have had last minute doubts. I could not leave it too long to decide, due to the fact Sylvia was to start her training that September of 1960. Here was my opportunity and I took it! So in the end we decided that I had nothing to lose by applying for this job as a clerk. This would be the first time I would work full time as a clerk since leaving school. My parents were astounded that I should procure such a position. They had great glee in telling the friends and neighbours, because most of them knew my history. Surely, they thought, something must be working for me, I could tell them what it was!

In the end it was Sylvia's father, who was the Branch Manager, who interviewed me and had to recommend me to Head Office. It was important for him to get this right, as if I failed it would look bad for him. It wasn't the fact of getting the job, but the ability to keep it that mattered. It was the challenge of it. You could say that I had a distinct advantage here, but as I have said, I had to make a success of it. I believe that God knew what He was doing in giving me that opportunity; I had to ensure that I made the most of it! So it was that I started working for the company on the 30th of September 1960. I was 22 years of age. My friends were thrilled for me! It reminded me of the verse in Philippians chapter 4:13: "I can do all things through Christ who strengthens me".

Chapter 6

Learning to trust

Before I met Sylvia, I often used to wonder if I would ever have the opportunity to meet someone and get married. Many questions would enter my mind - Who would want to marry me with all my baggage? What if I can't speak clearly enough? Would she accept the way I looked? There were so many doubts. I mean to say, whoever it turned out to be, she would be brave indeed! I suppose that because of all the difficulties experienced over the years with my operations and speaking problems, that one had to accept the possibility that I wouldn't get married. As it turned out, I needn't have worried, but I didn't know that at the time. You see, I was only looking at the situation from my standpoint, I had forgotten about the other person's angle. Naturally, I hoped that I would get married some day and that I had to be patient and wait and see what happened. My parents were doubtful and had difficulty in trying to encourage me one way or another, largely because they had the thought, "We don't think Mike will get married because of all his problems", but they didn't know the God that I knew and grew to trust.

I had been working amongst the young people for some time in the different roles and Sylvia was helping in some areas, also I would see her when meeting in the groups that I mentioned before from time to time. Now you will recall in chapter 5 that I started to 'go out' with Sylvia and that she decided to go into nursing training. This all happened in 1960 and it led to us becoming 'an item'.

I began to settle down in the new job as a clerk in the Assurance Society where Sylvia used to work. I said to myself, "I must make a real effort to succeed in this job". I began to be able to answer the telephone without being afraid! And to get to grips with talking to other members of the staff, agents and clients etc. I enjoyed the work as it included a great deal of figures and accounts, this was right down my street! The more I think about those days, the more I realised, I'm sure God has a sense of humour in placing me in an office like that. I learned a great deal about human nature and the different reactions people have in certain situations. This taught me how to react when I was faced with challenging circumstances and situations which I could not fully understand. I could study the different characteristics and reactions to scenarios that took place in the office, and they were many and varied. One can learn a lot about people by just listening to them and seeing how they handle difficulties. Then I would examine my own reactions when trying to put into words the things I was trying to say in given situations. Could I be positive? Could I make my listeners understand what I was saying without having to repeat myself? As far as I was concerned, I had to convince myself that I could pass the tests that were presented to me in the many different guises.

To backtrack a little, during 1961 Sylvia and I were

spending a lot more time together. I'd known her since I was 17 and, of course, we were friends throughout the time between 1956 and 1960. The more I thought of the possibility of asking Sylvia about getting engaged, the more I thought, perhaps she would turn me down. I mean, I wasn't the best looking chap in town, maybe she had got someone else already. I wasn't sure at the time. Eventually, I rustled up enough courage to at least pose the question. I was conscious that I lacked confidence, thinking she might turn me down, for whatever reason. However, I went for it! I think it was on one of those occasions when we were on a Mission outing to one of the beauty spots north of London, that I broached the subject of getting engaged soon. Sylvia at that point said regretfully, "No", not because of any of the thoughts that I had already thought about as to the reasons why she might turn me down, but for other reasons - she wanted to pursue her nursing training and travel. Needless to say, I was devastated, although I had partly expected this to happen. When I thought about it, I came to be convinced that Sylvia was the one for me, I was not interested in anyone else as far as marriage was concerned.

Although I went home feeling very sad, as you would expect, I still had the feeling, in a strange sort of way that all would be alright in the end. When I got home, I said nothing to my parents about what happened. I just felt I had to wait. I laid awake quite a long time that night, and somehow I had it in my mind that God would show me in the morning what His intentions were for me. I just felt this conviction that when I got up in the morning there would be a message for me. So I slept so much as I could. The next morning I woke with a sense of peace within me, went downstairs and picked up an envelope from just inside the front door. I picked it up gingerly and read the contents: "Come round as soon as you can". I think I broke all the records of getting from my house to hers! The answer was "Yes"! She would marry me! I was in shock and delighted. Basically the problem the day before was to do with her nursing commitment, but she preferred to get married. I know that God had had His hand upon our lives!

When I got home I felt able to tell my parents the good news. I know Mum was pleased for me but Dad was still a bit doubtful. During that June of 1961 we celebrated our engagement. We decided to get married the following May of 1962. I must say that when I told my parents that Sylvia was a manager's daughter, they were surprised and astounded, that I should meet someone like this and get married. As I said before, Mum was delighted, but Dad seemed to have reservations and did not seem so happy for some reason or other, he just said, "God help you" in such a way that he thought that I didn't know what I was doing. But God did. "Yes indeed, God will help me," I thought. Later, after the initial shock of the news about the marriage to them they did express their surprise about the course of events leading up to my announcement of the proposed marriage.

Mum and Dad were so surprised, finding that their son, for whom they didn't have too many hopes for the future, had not only found a job worthwhile doing, but was engaged to the "Boss' Daughter" and had far exceeded all their expectations. Well, I could have told them, God does not deal in half measures! I didn't say that to them, I just let events speak for themselves. It was probably to do with the fact they were not sure if I would be able to make a success of marriage or not and all the responsibilities that go with it. Thinking a little deeper about the situation as it appeared to my parents, I think Mum was afraid of what might happen if we had children, whether the children might have birth defects and such like. On reflection, I can understand her thinking, but it was based on what people would say in those days, not on medical considerations.

We planned to get married on May the 12th 1962. The folk at the Mission were highly delighted for us, as were all our friends and acquaintances. We decided to wait until then before getting married as Sylvia wanted to complete her training and qualify as an S.E.N (State Enrolled Nurse), which she did. Meanwhile I was coming to terms with my new job in the Insurance office. My family were very surprised that I was able to secure this position and would say how well I was doing to all their friends and neighbours. What a contrast to how they were reacting years before!

This was certainly a bit of a turn-a-round from early days of me trying to get any kind of job when leaving school. My parents must had realised something was going on in my life for me to be able to land on my feet in this way. Well, I could have told them, but I preferred to let the workings of my faith speak for themselves.

I had many lessons to learn during my teenage and twenties, there were many challenges to face as I sought to make progress in the various pursuits to do with my job and communication generally. I wasn't always successful, though! I had my moments when I would take for granted what people were doing for me and getting into bad habits with regard to my speaking etc. I knew I had to remain alert to this attitude, and correct myself when I fell short of what I desired, or others would correct me, and they often did so. On reflection, I am grateful for their patience and counsel. I share these things for one purpose: to assure you the reader, that if you have had to suffer physical defect, accident, or any other difficulty in your lives that prevents you living what I would term a 'normal' life there is help for you in your difficulties, even though from time to time you may fall short of your aims for one reason or another. It may be something you have forgotten or neglected to do, it doesn't matter what it is, it can be overcome. You may get annoyed with yourself or become frustrated because of the lack of progress you are making. 'Don't panic!' I've been there. Very often it is a case of 'one step forward and two steps backward' but you get there in the end.

Often the answer to some of these problems lies within the ability to overcome them ourselves, a lot depends on the determination of the individuals. Yes, there are some difficulties that we face, that require people who are trained in a special kind of way to help, but a lot of what we experience is helped by our co-operation with others who are trying to help us. Just sometimes, we may feel that we have the situation under control without asking for help, this can be a mistake! Let us think long and hard before we turn people away because we feel that our 'independence' is at risk. It is best to be reliant where we have to, than be independent and fail. I am so grateful to have had the privilege to receive help from my associates, friends and the professionals where this has been necessary, and the many who have persevered and spent time in finding solutions to some of my problems. I was told time and time again that it would be my determination not to be left behind, that would get me through, and they were right! You may be wondering, what in the world am I going on about? Let me tell you! We, who have had the experience of being born without the 'as seen on TV looks' or perhaps not being able to communicate with others as we would wish, have every right to live a full and useful life as everybody else, and we can do it! We may not necessarily do it in the same way as those we would call able-bodied, or perfectly formed, but in our unique way we can make that contribution to society which the world so badly needs. I know many of those who have served in the armed forces who have been injured profoundly, yet they are serving society in a most effective way, not letting their injuries stop them living a useful life. I take my hat off to them! I know that whenever I start to feel sorry for myself, I think of those in a worse position, and it puts everything into perspective. Why have I written this account? To share with you, that if I could overcome with the help of others in my life, some of the difficulties I have experienced, then you too can, with the help of others, overcome some of these difficulties. I can only hope and pray that you will be encouraged by what I have shared up to this point.

My advice to anyone going through times of difficulty, uncertainty or just a sheer lack of confidence, not necessarily because of physical impairment of disabilities, but many other conditions, such as: depression, trauma, psychological problems and other conditions that make you feel inadequate, don't despair! There are plenty of people who are willing and able to help you, plenty of good listeners who will spend time and effort to understand your problems, and if they don't, then they will refer you to someone who can understand your difficulties. We all need help on occasion, no-one is an island, and one should not be embarrassed or afraid to ask for help when the need arises. Again I thank God for all the help and advice I have received over the years from people who have put themselves out in order to get me through the difficult times, and there have been many! We often get the impression that the world doesn't care about people who are in any kind of need. This can be true, but equally true is the fact there are many who do care. There are many who we would call 'unsung heroes' who tirelessly help those who cannot get around as they would wish. The blood-donors who give of their time and blood to help those who need it for any reason. Or the volunteers who work for charities and such like. These people don't ask for reward for what they do. Some people may be reticent about coming forward to help, not because they don't want to, but because they may feel that they are not qualified to help. There are many who train to become a Samaritan, what an amazing organisation, what would we do without them? So many can be trained to help in given situations, depending on the need highlighted. In this world where there are so many symptoms of stress brought on by pressures of business and commerce and family life, and the need to make a living without getting into debt, caring for a family, and keeping a roof over one's head - you name it - these are all reasons why so many people get into stressful situations where their needs become so apparent. For those who, on top of all these problems, suffer invalidity, and difficulties in communication for any reason, or bear the results of accidents or birth defects, the world can seem a difficult place to be. All these problems tell us about the kind of world we live in. Sometimes there are no easy answers - they have to be worked out.

I leave to your imagination the problems I had to face when dealing with my peers, especially when I was at school from my earliest moments of awareness when starting school at six years of age at the hospital school in East Grinstead. The same was continued right through to when I left school at 15. Then came the challenges of starting work. This was a whole new ball game in so far as my relationships with other teenagers were concerned. I know that I had to trust God in every situation, I certainly could not manage these problems on my own. There were always those who, because of the way I looked in those days, thought I was a bit soft in the head as well, but I just had to get on with it. My brothers and sisters were surprised by the way people would treat me, they had to admit, they didn't understand how I could handle all this agro or what was the driving force behind my reactions to all the lack of understanding in others. They did their best to protect me, but there was only so much they could do. They couldn't be there all the time for me!

Despite all this, one thing that was paramount in my mind was, I would not be left behind. I wasn't going to be left floundering in a sea of disappointments and let down. I just hoped and prayed that they who taunted me and made fun, would one day come to realise that it was my faith that kept me going. It is often when people see how you cope in a difficult situation, that they question within themselves what makes this person tick. How can he/ she carry on despite all the opposition? I got this from people I was in conversation with many years later about the time they were the ones who used to taunt and make fun of people who they perceived to be less than themselves in various ways. I know for certain that I couldn't have achieved anything without the help I received from so many people. The experiences I went through prepared me for the work that I would be engaged in for most of my working life. It involved a great deal of contact with people; the complete opposite to what was expected of me when I was younger. I have shared these experiences, the circumstances of my birth, childhood, early teens and twenties, my marriage prospects and the jobs that I was able to secure. All this set against the background of seemingly insurmountable difficulties. There were other areas of experience in my life that presented further challenges, these I had to learn to overcome if I was to become a more complete person and be able to make an impact in the world of my experience. We would all like to see a society that is caring and compassionate, one which accepts those who are different from themselves, and yet allowing those who are affected by disability of any kind to present their own unique contribution to society. A society which tolerates those who, in the eyes of the world, are incomplete, and has patience and compassion for those less able than themselves.

It is quite a study to observe the reactions of people when faced with someone presenting a less than perfect image. The images we get when watching TV are of people who are beautiful, handsome and intelligent and generally have all their faculties. Often some people find it hard to face such people, largely, because they do not know what to say to them. They are embarrassed and lost for words, they only have to spot a slight physical flaw in their make-up, whether in speech, or the way they look, or indeed their mannerisms, in order for them to conclude that there is something more wrong than meets the eye. But there is no need for them to react this way. People with these troubles are only too happy for someone to speak to them, to show an interest in them and to be treated on equal terms as everyone else. Very often we would find that folk who are presenting these different images are quite capable in their own right, and we could be very surprised at the abilities these people possess. Why am I saying these things? Because I have witnessed so often the poor treatment and lack of real understanding that is shown towards people in this position. This is often the way life is, largely because we live in an insular world which is preoccupied with its own pursuits, and sometimes forgets the needs of others.

Throughout my life, as well as trying to communicate with those of my peers and working colleagues, I still had a life to live, to be able to talk to my friends and acquaintances and to stamp my identity on the world of my existence. This after all is all those of us who are affected in the ways described above want to do.

There were times when I thought I was not making myself understood sufficiently. It was down largely to my impatience at wanting to make more progress in my speaking efforts. I would go through times when I would say nothing to anyone. I would become frustrated because I could not communicate as I wanted to. My friends would say to me, "What's the matter Mike? Why are you not talking to us?" I would just mumble something to the effect, I didn't feel like it, but they knew me better than myself. They would sit there for ages trying to make me realise that all this takes time, and that I would get there in the end. I was grateful for their concern and eventually I would snap out of all this negativity. So you can see, the best of us have our moments of doubt, it's perfectly natural! This was the case before I got married. After I was married, somehow I didn't have time to dwell on my less than perfect speech, which was by the way now improving with practice and of course I had the encouragement of my wife and that of my friends. I was by this time gradually getting more confident when meeting people for the first time.

I began to accept more speaking engagements in various roles in local churches and Mission halls. This was a great opportunity to develop my speaking ability when speaking publicly. This is something that I never thought was going to be possible, as you would guess. It was at this point of my life, I began to realise what I had said to God, about speaking for Him if He enabled me to speak. It was not just a dream! It had become a reality. By the time I was 22, I was able to speak to my parents and make myself understood without too much effort. Mum and Dad commented on this fact as well which encouraged me greatly. At long last they found out I had a brain as well! It was, with the benefit of hindsight, understandable that they had doubts in the early days about my general abilities, so I don't blame them for that, although having said this, Mum always knew somehow I would make something of myself, but she didn't know how long it would take. My brothers and sisters used to encourage me by saying, "You're doing alright Mike, you'll get there", wherever 'there' was!

I have headed this chapter 'learning to trust'. It was extremely important for me to be able to trust people along the way of my journey. It was a difficult one, and I needed all the help I could get. I must say that without that help my journey would have been almost impossible to contemplate.

Chapter 7

Speaking Up

At last 1962 arrived. In fact I was looking forward to the 1st January 1962 and I was counting the days until I would be getting married. I must say the prospect of leaving home and setting up home on my own rather appealed to me. Actually Sylvia and I decided to get married on the 5th of May of that year, but following a plea by Sylvia's father we changed it to the 12th May. This was because Sylvia's father, George Goodman, was chairman of the Spurs supporters' club locally and wanted to go to the cup-final match at Wembley where Spurs were playing in the final. Now, we couldn't let him down could we! So we put off the wedding for one week, it seemed much longer that that at the time, but we were glad we did it because Spurs won that year. I was still astounded that Sylvia was willing to take me on, I felt she deserved a medal, I still do!

Just before we got married, I was considering yet another challenge that had been presented to me. It came in the form of a possibility of a job which would alter the whole course of my life. At that time, you will recall, I was working as a clerk in the assurance office, dealing with agents, staff and clients. Now, it just so happened that an agency would become vacant as the agent was coming up to retirement. He would retire in the August of 1962. The manager thought I was doing fine in the job as a clerk and was pleased with the way I was able to communicate with the agents and staff alike, so he spoke to me about the possibility of taking on an agency covering a certain area of London. He said, "Think about it whilst you are away on holiday and let me know what you feel when you get back". So I went off with Sylvia, on honeymoon actually! I had plenty to think about, wondering to myself if I could make a go of it. I discussed it with Sylvia quite extensively, because there was a lot to consider. I would be stepping out into the unknown to a large extent. There would be a great deal of talking in the job, as you would expect in a situation like this. Lots of things were whirling around in my head. Would I be jumping out of the frying pan into the fire? Should I be content to stay in the relative safe position as a clerk, or should I venture out on my own? I must say, that the whole idea of running an agency did appeal to me but could I do it and make a success of it? Needless to say we both considered the pros and cons and decided it was something of a challenge that had been put in my way. I felt at the time that my speech had improved to the point that I was not afraid to speak to people and could make myself understood without too many difficulties. Also I generally got on with folk, which would help me gain their confidence. Another area of consideration was my looks. Would I be acceptable, only time would tell. I simply had to trust God in the matter, after all, He would not had allowed this situation to arise had He thought I would not be able to cope. God knows us through and through!

To be honest, I never thought in a million years that I would be offered an opportunity like this! My conclusion was, the manager would not had offered this post to me if he thought I would not be able to cope, as I said, before I committed my answer to the manager for him to send to Head Office, I spoke to the leaders at the Mission where we both attended. Their response was one of surprise and pleasure for me. They said, "Mike, this is what faith is all about, stepping out into the unknown and trusting God for the future, go for it!" They were so pleased to realise that things were happening in my life that could not easily be explained. So Sylvia and I decided to launch out in this new venture, or adventure! There were some who were advising caution in view of my past, but then you always get them don't you? I finally came to the conclusion that this was a challenge I had to rise to. So on the following Monday, when I returned to work after our holiday, I confirmed it with the manager. He was delighted and put my application up to Head Office.

Whilst all this was going on and waiting for the response by Head Office, I had in my mind the seriousness of the situation and there were a number of considerations I had to bear in mind when making my decision to push ahead. Firstly, as a married man I had a responsibility to earn a living and keep my wife in the standard of living to which she had grown accustomed! No, not really, I'm just kidding! Sylvia was happy with whatever job I had. Also, I had to use this experience as a platform for future opportunities as and when they occurred, and I had to give God the opportunity to work out His will in my life, by using this experience in speaking to others, perhaps as a training ground for future service.

It was the beginning of June that my application went in, so I had to be patient and wait for them to respond. As the agent concerned was not retiring until the September, I just continued to do the present job I was engaged in for the time being. Whilst I was waiting, I thought it would be a good thing to get acquainted with certain aspects of the work I would be engaged in when the time came for me to take over the agency. Insurance can be quite a demanding occupation and there are many avenues to discover and get familiar with. This I was able to do during that three month waiting period. I often used to utter to others "I still haven't heard anything, how long will they take?" Others would answer, "Hang on in there Mike, it does take quite a time to decide on jobs like this." That was all part of my impatience coming out.

Many people I spoke to or knew me well, would say that because Sylvia's father was the manager of the insurance office, it was easy for me to get into a position as an Agent. I understood why they would had said this, but one thing they were forgetting was very vital in this scenario was that the manager was responsible for the success of the branch of the insurance society. Sylvia's father as manager had to recommend people for the various posts within the office and be sure that they would make a success of it, whatever the post was. So in the end it made very little difference to my prospects of being appointed or not. Head Office had to decide in the end. It certainly would have looked bad for the manager if anyone appointed fell on his face. So you see, the manager's reputation was on the line as well as mine. It couldn't have been an easy decision. I am eternally thankful for the opportunity given to me at that time, and I am very glad to say that it was a decision rightly made. As it turned out, I enjoyed the work and it was reflected in the moderate success I experienced as an agent and I gained a great deal of knowledge in the process. This is not to 'blow my own trumpet' but to underscore the truism that the world can have a mistaken view of what sort of people can be successful.

After waiting for what seemed an eternity, the day came when I finally heard from Head Office to say that I had been successful in my application and that I would be starting the work as an agent for the society on the 30th September 1962. I could only express one thing: "Praise God". I realised that this could not happen without Him. People were very pleased for me. When Sylvia and I told those at the Mission all about it, they were really pleased for us. Now it was down to me to make a success of it. I would not be able to blame anyone else if it didn't work out. There were others at the Mission who were encouraged in their own lives by what had happened in mine. So you never know what effect you can have on other people by the way you respond to what happens in your life. Others can be blessed by what you say and do in certain situations.

Even at this stage I was encouraging other people by telling them what has happened in my life. I didn't fully realise at the time just how much God would use me to encourage people who were going through difficulties, whatever they were in the future. Maybe it is the reason why I am writing this account of my life. I do sincerely hope and pray that this account called 'The Words of my Mouth' will create the desire in many to seek help and counsel whenever they feel the need. To know that there are those 'out there' who are willing and able to help. Don't struggle on your own for no good reason. "It's good to talk". A problem shared is a problem halved.

I was really looking forward to starting my experience as an agent. I must say though, I had a few butterflies in my stomach at the thought of it all. I thought at the time "Is this really me?" I just couldn't get my head round the fact I was to be the agent for that particular area. I did start to feel the sense of responsibility as the time grew nearer to when I was due to begin the work.

At last I started to work on the agency, and I enjoyed the work. What a tremendous opportunity it presented to develop my speaking skills, but I had to work at it! As I grew in confidence, I found I became reasonably successful in further developing the size of the business on my books. I do believe, on reflection, this success was largely due to my own attitude to the job and how I dealt with people generally. Once people got to know me, I became a friend and confidante to them. I found that I was building up a pool of knowledge about people and situations. I sought to take interest in my clients and genuinely tried to help them in their financial planning and decision making. I felt it a privilege to be in such a position and often people would be glad to see me, especially the older people. Some of them didn't have visitors from one month to another and they would be glad of a chat. I was also thankful that I could indeed chat to them after all my difficulties in communication when I was younger. As I got to know people and they me, they would share all sorts of problems, without me asking or inviting them to share. Problems like filling in forms which they could not understand and needed help with. Even among younger people this would occur! I was glad to be able to help because this only served to build up confidence and even as a bi-product procure further new business. So it worked well for all of us!

Whilst all this was going on, we had moved to Ilford (Redbridge). After about a year and a half there, we were going to a Baptist church where they had a large Sunday school and needed more teachers. I was invited to take a class and I was glad of the opportunity once again to share with them. At this time they were in the process of taking the children through the Scripture Union Examinations. We had to train the children to the point whereby they could sit the examination and we would be reasonably happy that they would pass. I most enjoyed this aspect of the work. This became very exciting when the results were finally through and we could see the children's faces when they were told they had passed the examination. It made it all worthwhile. I was almost as excited as they were! I always feel so much of the privilege of talking to anyone about God's word, as I remember what God's promise to me was.

It is such a privilege to be able to talk to people, I suppose I feel this way because of the journey I have made with regard to my communication difficulties. But they are behind me now to a large extent. I was so glad that I had reached the point of not worrying too much over how I was coming over to those I was addressing. It made all the difference to me to be able to speak in such a way that people could understand me the first time without them having to say, "I'm sorry, would you repeat that". It can be very tiring!

I had, over the course of time, been developing my office and communication skills. It was becoming more important to develop these skills with the event of the computer and electronic typewriters, and calculators. Now I sought a situation whereby I would be able to put to use these skills. It wasn't that I had itchy feet or that I couldn't settle down for any length of time in a particular job. It was the fact I didn't possess a means of transport at the time and it became difficult for me to get round to all the clients on my book. I still wanted to be occupied within the insurance world which I found to be interesting. My desire was to be in a position of responsibility for other working colleagues. After nearly two years on the agency and having no transport, I decided it would be better for me to go over to the administrative side of the business.

An opportunity came for me in the shape of what was known in those days as the position of Principal Clerk (Chief Clerk). By now I was 24 years old and the job became vacant through retirement. The manager realised that without a means of transport, it would be difficult to run the agency, although not impossible! The area I covered was fairly consolidated, but still a large area to cover gradually throughout the week. Knowing this, he approached me as to whether I would be interested in making the switch. I thought this was very good of him. He didn't want to lose me as an agent, because I had been reasonably successful. Now, the fact of Sylvia's father being the manager was not going to have any influence in connection with my application for the position this time. The vacancy had arisen in another part of London where I did not know anyone. Whatever way some people viewed the situation when I applied for the agency, this was going to be a completely new ball game! I viewed my experience on the agency as gaining valuable knowledge of the business, in order that when in a position of checking the administrative side of the agents' accounts, I would be aware of all that is involved on that side of things.

The duties of a Principal Clerk were many and varied. The responsibilities included: looking after the agents' accounts; the other clerks; all financial matters; auditing; payment of salaries; plus the responsibility for payment of claims to policy holders. There were quite a lot more areas, which I cannot go into, needless to say, I would be kept very busy. I relished the challenge that this new position held for me. Believing I'd built up sufficient experience to cope with the job, I applied to Head Office to be considered. I left it to God to sort this out for me. Again I had to be patient for it was another three months before the person was to retire. Sylvia and I had discussions about the changes this would bring upon us. We thought if this was God's will then He would make it plain. I had learned to speak more clearly as time went on, and I just hoped that I had made sufficient progress in that area. I was still involving a lot of talking! Talking! Talking! One had to be prepared!

So whilst I was awaiting for the time to pass, I began to study more about Insurance Law and Practice. This knowledge would be vital if I was appointed, there's nothing lost in being prepared! I enjoyed attending the local college where people were studying for the ACII (Chartered Insurance Institute) certificate and covering the various modules such as: Industrial life, Marine and General Branch Insurance. I didn't necessarily cover all these, my main areas were General Household and Life. I believed that this would help me in my understanding and my approach to the job I was applying for. I did wonder how long it would be before I would be told if I had got onto the 'short list' for people who would be interviewed.

Towards the end of August 1964 I heard from Head Office that I would indeed be on that short list. I was surprised to get this far because, secretly, I did have doubts as to whether I had sufficient experience to hold this position. Finally the day came in the first week of that September, I had to attend interview in Liverpool. Of course, I would say to myself I was only on the short list and that they wanted to make up the numbers! I also thought to myself "O ye of little faith!' There was I, so I thought I stood very little chance with this lot! As it turned out, I was the last to be interviewed, so I had to sit right through waiting for everyone to be interviewed, by the time they got to interview me, they would be exhausted. "Could I make an impression?" I said to myself.

The interview itself went quite well considering, except for one thing I said in answer to a particular question on fidelity. I stated "As a Christian, honesty is a pre-requisite in any situation where finance is involved, as indeed in all situations, trust is placed in me, therefore I would honour that trust." I came away from that interview thinking "What did I have to say that for?" I thought I'd blown it! When I got home, Sylvia asked me how I had got on. After sharing with her some details of how it went, I said, "Well! I think I did OK". You can never be absolutely sure about these things, you just have to wait and hope that it will turn out to your advantage. I decided that I would not dwell on the subject because in my opinion it would be a waste of time and energy worrying about something that may or may not happen. Again I had to trust God in the situation, there was nothing more I could do. I must admit to laying awake some nights thinking if only I had said this or that at the interview or regret saying certain things which could make all the difference in the outcome. It was all rather silly, but people do this sort of thing! Well, Sylvia said, "Forget it for now, don't worry."

My parents thought I should be content with what I was already doing, rather than put myself through this ordeal. I didn't consider it an 'ordeal' but it was a challenge!

About two weeks later I heard from HO that I had not got the job I was interviewed for but, much to my surprise, they were offering another position! It would be doing the same tasks, but in a much larger branch office with a lot more responsibility. I was astounded! I needed someone to pinch me to see if I wasn't dreaming. What's that about giving God the honour and he honours you? I didn't realise it at the time, but that is what happened at the interview. It was my answer to the question about fidelity and honesty that, I was later to be told, was the reason why the interview board felt they could offer me the branch in central London. People were so surprised and pleased for me.

I took up my duties in the central London branch in the October and I remained there until the Society closed that office for consolidation purposes and we were all transferred to a much larger area office in Redbridge, Ilford. Instead of 23 Agents and three staff, I had 42 agents and seven staff that I was responsible for under a district manager. This was quite a challenge, but one I was willing to face up to. The tasks were the same but on a much larger scale than before. I would occasionally take stock in myself as it were and wondered "Is this really me?" When I explained to my friends and family what was involved in this job, they were dumbfounded - how could someone like me get into a position like this? Like others I was truly amazed, you see, with God, nothing is impossible!

It had been considered by my parents, with the best will in the world, that I could be described as a 'no-hoper', certainly when you think about the prospects or lack of them when I left school and here I was with all this responsibility! Others were amazed at what had happened, and again were telling people how well I was doing. I was pleased for them, because I ceased to be the source of embarrassment and they could actually have a sense of pride in their son, who had risen from the state of having little to shout about, to being someone that had made a name for himself. This, of course, was from the other people's point of view. I remain humble at the thought that I am here by the grace of God. He has been my inspiration right from the start.

You will recall that earlier in this account I shared with you my experiences when going out from the Mission with a group of young people to take services in various places in north London, with different people taking various parts in the service. This proved good experience for many and brought out the 'hidden talents' of individual team members. You will also recall that I said the first time I took a service on my own was at the 'Welcome Mission'. That was indeed a special occasion for me! I was conscious of my inadequacy but I knew it marked a turning point in my life as far as speaking was concerned. There would be further opportunities to speak at various church groups at that time.

When I look back, I can see how easy it would have been for me just to give up and shrink back from venturing into service for God or man because of my impediment. People would have understood and not expected me to make much effort to improve myself or make determined efforts to learn to speak more clearly. Had I gone down that road, there would have been no point to my life. I would have just drifted through life hoping for the best but expecting the worse. I would have felt it was no use trying to beat myself up for no good reason and just somehow get through life as best I could without too much hassle. I am glad that I didn't take that attitude! I find certain people would not have been too surprised if that had been the case. So why did I take the opposite view and approach? I may have looked different from other people, but inside I was the same as others, therefore there was no reason why I should have given up. Once I become a Christian, I realised that I had a job to do, and it was not to be in my own strength. God had promised to enable me to overcome the very real difficulties that I was to experience in my life. The transition from being viewed as someone who looked different and spoke differently from everyone else, to becoming someone who would become able to communicate and look pretty much the same as everyone else, was to take time. This would take a lot of patience and belief.

What I have been able to overcome with the help of others, I believe can be overcome by anyone who has or is suffering similar difficulties in their lives as I have. I want to encourage you in this! I have not found this an easy journey, but it has been rewarding. I haven't reached the goal yet but I'm getting there. This is what this account has been about, being 'over-comers'. Let us speak the words, first from the heart, then from our mouths.

I am always conscious of all the help being afforded me over the years in so many directions. Folk would look at me sometimes and wonder where I'm coming from! With all the troubles I have had over the years they thought I would be somewhat reticent or laid back but somehow it seemed to be the reverse. I know one thing, faith means nothing if you do not take that first step of believing and trusting God. When one does this, one puts oneself in God's hands. God needs hands and mouths, sometimes you have those hands and mouths that God wants to use. I have had the privilege of meeting people who have suffered terribly because of illness or disability and yet they have displayed remarkable resilience in the face of seemingly hopeless odds. They have been able to rise above their limitations and inspire those around them with their cheerfulness and sheer determination to live life to the full. I salute them! They have encouraged me. Some cases I saw when I was in hospital in my early days were horrific and yet they did not complain, they just got on with getting better and back to some form of normality. They had determination, and I'm sure this attitude helped them to face the future, whatever it would have brought them.

Chapter 8

Further Challenges

I remained in this position for the next three years, enjoying the work, but finding it increasingly demanding. I had a lot of responsibility and more and more was being laid upon me, so after careful consideration I decided to seek wider experience in the general field of Insurance, including Life, Marine and Motor. This meant that I had to seek employment with another company, as the present company did not cater for general insurance needs, only for life assurance needs. So after looking around I began to feel that it would be a good move to become 'the man from the 'well known company' and because of my experience I was accepted. I'd always had a high regard for the image of those working for such an august company, but I never thought I would be working for them. I met very different people in my work, and found that I could converse with people from all walks of life, it was interesting that I could communicate with them at all levels. There was so much to learn, even about the different agencies one could hold with this company, I did manage to get on quite well and procure new business. This was to be in striking contrast to the limitations I experienced with my previous employment, where one was not permitted to hold other agencies. It's a bit technical, but that is how it worked in those days. So I appreciated the wider scope this gave me and spent the next two and a half years with this company. Because of the 'image' of this company, I was surprised I actually worked for them and I was glad they gave me the opportunity to do so, having in my mind, not necessarily in theirs, the way I looked. A lot was down to the local manager in giving me that opportunity to prove myself. I learned a great deal in having to deal with all sorts of situations, people and handling many different types of claims etc. I must admit, that there were times when I wondered how on earth I had got myself into this kind of occupation, bearing in mind the difficulties I'd had during the earlier part of my life. People not only began to understand me, having got used to my speaking, but often they confided in me over various matters as I went round on the agency. It wasn't only insurance that I found myself helping people with, often I would be asked to help people fill in forms for tax, post-office and other things. I actually used to do this when working for my previous company as I have said before. I did find that in doing this, that this helped people to be able to talk to me on a more friendly basis as well as dealing with them as clients. Because of the wider scope that this job offered, it enabled me to meet more people with the different areas of interest. You may be wondering why I took on another agency, bearing in mind that I left my previous agency due to lack of transport. Well, in this case the company I was now working for had organised the agency on a more consolidated basis, this meant that the calls were closer together and could be serviced by planning them on a walking basis. Occasionally I would use a motorbike, but I didn't need that really.

By 1968 Sylvia and I had been married for six years and we were still waiting to have our first child. There was no reason as far as we were concerned as to why we could not have children, so we thought it advisable for Sylvia to go through a series of test and examinations just to check that everything was o k. In the end, there was indeed no problem. Many couples go a few years without having children, but we felt a little concerned about the situation. We decided to approach the then Baptist Adoption Society (This no longer exists) to see if they could help us and accept us on their waiting list. After going through the necessary formalities we were accepted and just waited. The time came when they wrote to us with the news that they had a baby from appropriate background which they would like us to consider.

We had thought that because at the time, we lived in a flat that they wouldn't necessarily respond so quickly to our request, although when an official came to interview us and view our accommodation and circumstances, she thought is very amusing when she observed the antics of our dog and cat playing together. Maybe this was a help in that if we had patience and care for these animals, then perhaps, the Society would see that as a good sign of the care we would exercise over the bringing up of a child. So it was in the December of 1968 we received the offer of a child. Then, lo and behold, just at that time we realised we were expecting our own child! I'm told this does happen from time to time! We were completely bemused and happy, but what do we do about the Adoption Society? We contacted them, and they were very pleased for us and said that they would keep our name on their books in case we wanted to adopt at a later stage. My thoughts were, that God wanted the best for us, He knew our needs and we shall be for ever grateful to Him.

Just back-tracking a little. During the summer of 1968 I found myself beginning to feel a little uncomfortable with what was taking place in the insurance industry. I was not happy with some of the practices they were introducing and requiring us to do as agents. Gradually I became disillusioned and dissatisfied with the job as some of the practices were questionable against my values as a Christian. I hasten to add, this was my own personal and considered opinion. I decided it was time to make a change of direction and seek work where I could use my many skills that I had acquired to better and more satisfying effect.

At this time also, Sylvia's parents decided to move to Devon, following the retirement of her dad. They decided to have a bungalow built for themselves in Exmouth and were looking forward to settling down in their new surroundings. This caused Sylvia and me to contemplate a possible move to Devon to be near them and to enjoy that part of the country.

There were very few relatives living nearby to where we lived in Ilford, so we saw very little of them anyway. We no longer attended the Mission in Tottenham as it was too far to travel to on a Sunday. We did, however, attend a Baptist Church in the immediate area and we enjoyed the fellowship. However, we had not made that many close friends so it felt right about making the decision to leave for pastures new. I was quite a challenge, in that I was to leave my present employment and try to find something else when we moved down to Devon. This would prove to be a temporary position as I wanted to really find the right job that once again would give me job satisfaction. By this time my experience would be in commercial/office administration and sales - certainly working with people and doing something worthwhile.

There were a number of considerations in all this. We didn't know anyone in Devon, which in itself would prove to be a step of faith; we also had to sell our lovely flat reasonably quickly, and we didn't know what the housing market was like in Exmouth where we were going to live, or hoped to live! We came to the conclusion that if we didn't make the move then we might possibly lose our opportunity whilst we were still young enough to start again. Much to our surprise, we did sell quite quickly in an otherwise slow market. This was another indication that it was the right thing to do.

Sylvia was expecting her first child and on July 16th Lisa arrived. This put us in an 'interesting' situation, because we could not purchase or rent a property in Devon as we were not there yet, and would had been too much of a risk to go by estate agents' recommendations merely on their say so. I could not afford to make prior visits to test the grounds as it were. We had ideas of what the place was like though from visiting whilst on holidays sometimes. The contracts were signed with the new owners of our flat and we finally found ourselves on a train coming down to Exmouth in the August of 1969. We must have been a curious sight as we travelled with Lisa, our three-week old daughter, a dog and a cat in a basket! Not in the same basket I hasten to add! Forgive me! I always see the funny side of things like this.

We had arranged to dwell with Sylvia's parents in Exmouth until we found a place of our own. As I have stated, they had a bungalow built for themselves with plenty of room, and I helped to convert a space under the bungalow into a room, and there was sufficient space for all our furniture we brought with us, so it was a handy space for us to occupy for sleeping purposes and privacy whilst we were able to have meals upstairs with Sylvia's parents. What was really nice was that from any of the rooms at the rear of the bungalow, we had a view over the park.

On the Monday morning, following our move from Ilford, I didn't waste any time, I went out looking for work. There was a medium size engineering firm making tools for the plastics industry, and I was able to get a temporary job there whilst waiting to find a more suitable job as I have said.

As it turned out it was an interesting job, far more so than I had anticipated. It made a change from what I was used to, and I think it helped to broaden my mind as far as occupations were concerned. You meet different types of people in a situation when people are working close together. We certainly were working to very fine measurements and had to be very precise. I found this to be quite demanding and a totally new experience. It is surprising what one can learn about people in these situations! I had to learn not to write off any experience as not important. I spent getting on for two years in total working for this engineering company and as a clerk for a company which installed heating systems etc. In all this, I never lost sight of what I really wanted to do, I just had to wait for that opportunity to come along.

During this period, our second child was born in the January of 1971. We were thrilled about this because we now had our own place nearby. It was a maisonette and we had a bit more room to get everything in and put our own stamp on our accommodation. After waiting for six to seven years for our own child, we now had two children born within the space of one and a half years! Marion was the most recent to arrive on the scene. She was born at home.

Not long after Marion came along, I was still looking for that ideal work situation. I decided to apply for a job advertised by the local Electricity Board in Exeter (as it was then known). They wanted someone to work in their planning department. A little later, I was to discover that they had about 30 applicants for the job and they were those who knew the locality and live in the area. That I thought would give them a distinct advantage over me. However, I pressed on with the interview preparation. When the time came for me to appear on the 'short list' much to my surprise I duly went to the interview and just trusted God in the matter. I must have created the right kind of impression because I was appointed as a clerk in the department. This of course, was only my first step on a rather tall ladder. The work was interesting enough, but it had its limitations and I found it lacked challenge and promotional possibilities.

I settled down in the knowledge that I would keep my eyes open for other openings within the Board; at that time there was a wide diversity of activities and business within the company, so it would be worthwhile waiting for the right thing to come along. About a year later, I was reading the notice board one day just scouring through the list of vacancies in case there was something I might be interested in. I did spot a vacancy in Exmouth for a senior sales person to man the service-centre. I thought, as I preferred to deal with the public directly this position would be a good start with my experience in sales and administration, plus the fact it would mean I would not have to travel, as I lived not very far from the centre. At last I saw this as an opportunity to use my brain, if I could locate it! So I applied for the job, I had nothing to lose. I still had my job with the Board, so my income was safe, I did have a mortgage at the time, so I had to act in a responsible way. One thing for sure, with this vacancy, everyone and their grandmother would be applying, it's quite understandable, who wouldn't want to come to this part of the country, to this environment to work?

It looked unlikely that I would be successful on this occasion. But after waiting a while, I heard from the office, that I had made the 'short list' once again. It was now mid July 1971 and I was 33 years old. All the while I was waiting to go for the interview I kept thinking to myself that there would be many other employees working for the Board who would dearly love to come down to this part of the country to work. I mean! Exmouth was and is a very nice place to live and work.

The day of the interview finally came. I found that I was the penultimate person to be 'grilled'. I did my best to make the right impression, remembering what happened several years before when I was interviewed for that Chief Clerk's job with the Assurance Society's branch office. This job didn't just deal with sales etc. but was a responsible position where I would be dealing with all sorts of situations and handling customers' concerns, electricity accounts and appliances and advising them on the use of electricity generally. The question of fidelity arose again! So I gave the same answer as I did all those years before. I had to convince the panel that I could do the job. I hoped my speech was now acceptable as for any other person applying for the position.

Once the interview was over, I was told that it would be about a week before I would learn the result. What a week that was! As I have said, patience is not my strong point. However, it was rewarded when I received the letter from the Board that I had been successful in my application. Later I was told by the person who was to become my manager, that there were over 100 applications and then ten picked for the short-list. Well! I was really shocked to hear that. When I told Sylvia, she was very pleased indeed for me. She knew I preferred this kind of work instead of just sitting behind a desk. It was a 'hands on' situation and I was going to give it my fullest attention.

I did just hope that when I met the rest of the staff that they would accept me for who I was and not be influenced by the way I looked. My looks were considerably better by now, than ten years earlier. I needed not to have been concerned as the people were great! Sometimes we worry over things that may or might not happen, don't we!

During the first four years working for the Electricity Co we added another child to the family, Paul in 1973 (Oct). I remember what Mum used to say to me about having children, maybe this is what was behind their feelings of lack of enthusiasm when talking about getting married. They were afraid that there might be something wrong with the children because of what happened in my case. They needed not to worry, all of them were perfectly formed. I think that 'old wives' tales' might have influenced them. In those days people had all sorts of ideas, which possibly could get out of hand if you were not careful. When I got married to Sylvia, I was quite relaxed about this problem, because I felt in myself that everything would be alright, so did Sylvia. Not only did they grow up and become parents themselves, but all the grandchildren are fantastic. So we are grateful to God for this! All the rest of my family are really pleased how it turned out for Sylvia and myself.

Funnily enough, our children have grown up and taken after Sylvia and myself in so many ways, to the extent of being interested in similar kinds of work and other interests. I suppose that is natural, but, none-the-less it is gratifying to know that they are very capable people in themselves. I am grateful to God that none of what I suffered as a child has affected them in the slightest way.

I had been working for the Board as a senior sales person in the Service Centre for about five years and during the period I was receiving training by attending several courses at the training centre in Bristol. I took further courses as time went on in particular areas. Altogether I spent about five years doing this. I had to be able to pass the necessary exams if I wanted to make progress in job management. The courses were many and varied, but were hard work, and fun! Well, anything worth doing is not necessarily easy is it? It was an absolute necessity to pass these exams to prove to the company that I would be able to take on management of a branch, and I was determined to get through this somehow. No-one ever achieved anything without hard work, and I was no different to anyone else!

About two years after this period of training was completed and I had the necessary qualifications to move on to a better position, if the opportunity came along, I settled down to the task at hand, to make a success of the position I held with the company. Now round about this time changes were being made in the structure and organisational aspects of the business, mainly to do with the running of the service centres and shops. The management decided to open 'superstores' in the Devon area and upgrade where possible the look of the retail outlets. I had attained the main qualification: The Electricity, Sales and Utilisation certificate under the auspices of the Electricity Council this enabled me to move up to supervisor of the branch I was already in. I would be able to apply for management when the opportunity arose. By the end of this process I had completed four years in my position as Supervisor. I was visited one day by the retail manager who informed me that I would become the manager of the branch. I was delighted and willing to face up to the challenge. I spent the next thirteen years in that position.

To add further responsibilities to my remit, I became responsible for the training of up-and-coming managers. I enjoyed this aspect of the work and felt it a privilege to be engaged in this teaching role. We made a move as a centre to a much larger unit in a new precinct. This proved to be very useful and a much better situation for both staff and customers alike.

During 1992, after what was known as privatisation had taken place within the electricity industry, my centre, together with a number of others on the retail side of the business, was being closed. Most of the business was being transferred to the existing large superstores. So after 21 years with the Board I found myself placed on the redundancy programme. When I think back to those days, I must say I wasn't particularly sad. Yes, I would miss the comradeship of my colleagues and contacts with the general public with all their problems and challenges but we had to move on, after all, I could do something else. I received my redundancy notice whilst I was in hospital having a hernia operation. That seemed a good 'send off' at the time! There wasn't a great deal I could do about this and after just over 21 years in the job and at the age of 54 it was a bit early for retirement.

During the two years before I was made redundant I had developed type 2 diabetes and was not in the best of health generally. So I thought it was the right time for all these things to happen anyway. I considered my self blessed indeed to have been able to spend over 21 years with the same employer; a lot of people would be glad to have that kind of security in these days! It's amazing when you consider that in the 60s and 70s you could walk out of one job and into another without too much trouble at all. I do feel sorry for the youngsters these days as they face getting permanent employment so as to be able to set up home and raise a family. For those on the dole, I cannot imagine what they must feel the future holds for them.

Sylvia and I discussed what our options were. At the age I was, it would be difficult, to say the least, for me to get another job. There was a lot of 'ageism' about where would-be-employers were not prepared to take on the 'more mature' applicants for jobs, as they saw it as a waste of time just for the sake of 10 or 15 years' investment at the most. This is still a problem with many. There are only a few exceptions. Some of the larger food stores take on 'shelf-stackers', minimum wage earners.

As for me, once I left the Board, I felt just to sit back and never bother to find another job would be a big mistake! Ok, I was not in the best of health, but I could still use my brain! I wasn't senile. I have seen many people just give up and become bedraggled, depressed and not look after themselves because they had been made redundant, and felt as though they had been confined to the scrap-heap. This was not going to happen to me! That same old determination was rearing its head in me again. You could say that I'd had a lot of practice at this! I had developed this attitude over the years, born out of my experiences and difficulties. I simply had to rise above this 'give up' type of reaction and remain positive. Going round wearing a 'poker' face wasn't going to help me find another job was it? I went along to the local employment office (it was called at the time) to enquire about a job or, if not, any courses in the area of I.T that I could go on. I had been used to the use of computers in my last job from an operational standpoint. I always found it interesting. This was an opportunity to get to know a bit more about that side of things as well as studying other subjects.

At the time of my enquiry, the colleges were running courses for those in poor health or disabilities, so that they could be retrained to do other kinds of work. I asked the agency to put me on the list of those applying, but first I had to take an entrance examination to assess the kind of work potential I possessed. I took the exam and thankfully it was no problem. Eventually I was accepted on to the programme for NVQs and the RSA courses. I did a number of courses at the same time - I must have been off my head! They were intensive courses and I had to stick with it because they were quite demanding for an 'olden like me! As it happened, I studied the following: Computer Accounts, Manual Accounts, Word Processing, Business Administration, A Level Business, English, and I.T. generally. In order to be able to concentrate on all this work, I stayed at the college during the week and just came home for weekends. This was a rough time for me as it was the first time that I had been separated from Sylvia for any length of time. I'd been on courses, as I have said, but they would only be for a week at a time. I suppose it all took about a year and a half to get through. Much to my surprise I did manage to pass all the exams with first class passes included. I was amazed!

Now I say all this, not to blow my own trumpet, but because I am not an academic. If I can do this, then other people can as well. When I was at college, I used to say to myself, "What on earth am I doing?" I was surrounded by project papers all over the place, pinned up on the walls of my room, so that I could work more easily on them. I often found myself encouraging other people who were finding it tough going as well, and we helped each other along the way. This is how life should be!

Chapter 9

Amazing Grace

Once all this study was out of the way I began looking for work in the hope that I could put into practice the things that I had learned. I went off to the employment agency again, but as before, they had nothing to offer. I think on reflection, they were up against ageism and considered it too much to expect an employer to take me on at my age. I was now 56, but I was not prepared to just let it go at that. I had to keep filling in those wretched forms that the job centre required in order to prove that one had been looking actively for work, otherwise you would not be entitled to unemployment benefit or 'job seeker's allowance'. I thought to myself "I am not going to put up with all this nonsense for long!" So I searched the papers continually until one day I found something that looked promising and might be just the thing.

I phoned the number and spoke to the manager who, to my surprise, invited me along for an interview. By now it was a few weeks since leaving college. I took along my validated certificates to show evidence of my studies. The job entailed working as a depot clerk programming all the driver's work requirements. In this case it was a food distribution depot for a well-known provisions manufacturer. It was all computer work, carrying out checks and examining the accounts of the drivers. It was quite involved in some aspects of the work. So I sat through the manager's appraisal of what my duties would be, thinking, "I wonder if he will offer me this job or not?" I was astounded, when he suddenly said, "When can you start?" I said, "As soon as possible." I started the job on the following Monday. I was absolutely thrilled and so was my wife. I didn't think I had done too bad getting a job at my age. I did go back to the employment agency to let them know that I had found a job without their help, but they were very pleased for me.

There was a great deal of information that I had to take on board, as you would with any new job, but in this case, I would be using the new technology that I had gained at college for the first time in actual practice. The title of my job had slightly altered, because I was also called the security officer to add to my list of souvenirs! It just served to illustrate the complexity of the job in hand. I did eventually get into the job quite well and had things running reasonably smoothly including the computer forward-planning requirements. I found this all very interesting, as I had continued contact with all the driver/salesmen and management in the course of my daily work. I did find that I brought into use all the different aspects of my experience, with regard to my speaking, confidence and determination; this enabled me to move forward and establish good working relationships with all those with whom I came into contact. There is little doubt that all the lessons of the past had come into their own at this point in my quest to rise above the difficulties that I had faced earlier in my life. I always say, "If I can do these things, then others should attempt them". I'm no different.

It felt really good to be in work again; at least I was making a contribution to the running of our household expenses and not having to rely on the state. Although I spent the minimum time on benefits, I didn't like that idea at all and I couldn't go on in that way. In that short period, I felt as though I had lost my identity somewhat, now I could be myself again. There is a sense of pride in managing your own life, without having to rely on others unnecessarily. God knew all about my thoughts on this subject and He expected me to co-operate with Him in finding the answers to situations like these. I could have sat back and waited for someone to come and offer me a job, but that was not going to happen! I had to do something myself. In this way God gave me the ability to do whatever it took to remedy the situation. All we have to do is to trust in the Almighty in every circumstance of life, you will not be disappointed! When one prays about a matter, don't automatically think that the answer will come exactly as you have requested in the way you expect, there are many ways that prayers are answered. Just sometimes the answer may be 'No' not because God does not listen or care, but because He cares. If we are believers, He wants the best for us. Sometimes what we pray for is not right for us. Often prayers are answered in a totally different way to what we expect.

Once having settled down in the latest job, I was able to concentrate on other interests, and all the time I was aware that the experiences I had been through helped me to be able to communicate with others in the course of my church associations. I still find it difficult to realise that God enabled me to hold certain positions within the church (mainly Baptist) fellowships. To this day, I never cease to be amazed how God could use me in these situations. I know, without Him I would be unable to do anything. Perhaps God was preparing me for this work throughout the years in my experiences and how I have been able to deal with the difficult issues that have arisen in my life. After all, how would I had been able to have empathy for someone going 'through the mill' if I had not had any of these experiences? So I am thankful to God for the difficult times as well as all the good and pleasurable times, and there have been many! I never thought I would say this! I thank God for the way I was born. This seems an odd thing to say, especially because of all the trouble it caused me throughout the years. Looking back, I can see the possible reasons why I had to go through this. I certainly wouldn't like anyone else to experience this problem, and some people have far more serious problems in their lives. But the hope is that there will be someone who will support us by showing care and giving encouragement just at the time we need it. Most people, when I have shared with them something of my story are surprised that I am still here to tell the story. They often comment, "I don't know how you survived all that trouble". It's then I tell them how I did survive! In answer to their question, I share with them the fact that God plays a big part in my life and that all that has happened to me has been overcome through my faith in Him. If it weren't so I would had been cast down into oblivion years ago. My testimony is that God worked through me despite my shortcomings, and I have plenty of them! Maybe you too will come to realise that there is someone there to help you too to overcome the difficulties that you face in your lives! I have found this to be so, so can you!

I'm just an ordinary fellow, whom God loves, and this makes the difference. God loves you too as you are. There's an old hymn that starts so: "Just as I am, thine own to be". That tells a very important story. God loves you just as you are! If you come to Him in faith believing what He has done for you (John 3:16-18) then He has promised to care for you and be with you at all times, even in the tough times. He has not promised to protect us from natural occurrences nor being treated badly by others, but He has promised to be with us in these circumstances. Very often bad experiences can have the effect of building up our characters and our strength to meet the demands the world makes on us from time to time. We are trained to help others in such a way. The question "how can we or I help" comes into its own at such a time when it can be vitally important to the other person. The "can we or I help?" becomes more positive when we can say "how can we help?" Having had different experiences, we can offer that question with greater confidence. At such times we can ask for discernment or wisdom in differentiating between the right or wrong paths to tread in any particular case, this can only come through experience.

Going back to when Sylvia and I had settled in Exmouth, we started attending the Baptist Church where we quickly settled down to the routine of Sunday worship and midweek activities. We discovered from the start that the church had an outreach project. This was to build a daughter church on the outskirts of the town. There was a group of people who were especially set aside to pray for God's leading in this area. This ultimately lead to the forming of a house-group within the area that the church was to be built. After a while we gained the use of a primary school where we could hold our meetings and start a Sunday school class. In this way we were able to gather together a nucleus of foundational members of the new church once it had been built. This nucleus consisted of about seventeen people and involved a good number of residences in the area - these we used for the house-groups. I was responsible for arranging the speakers and venues. Once the building was ready, which would have been around 1973, we all moved into the new church. We were so glad that all the cost had been covered through the very generous and sacrificial giving of many people. I believe that any project worth its name is based on good preparation and groundwork. Not only for a building but the people themselves!

When the occasion of the opening of the new church arrived, a minister who was specially invited to speak used the following topic for his talk: "Christianity is working with your jackets off and your sleeves rolled up". I took that on board! There is no doubt about this truism. The practical issues of getting the job done involves all aspects of the work: practical, spiritual, planning, and application. This all applies when we are in a position to help others on the road of life. What then is first? Let's take the last one first; planning. When I was looking at the field where the building was to take place, I found I was looking at mounds of weeds, thorns and every other kind of growth imaginable. Somehow this field had to be prepared! Just prior to the starting of the build, I found myself treating the field with a chemical weed-killer. This was a very strong mixture, but was necessary to prepare the ground. The ground had to be in a very good state, so that the foundation could be built without any snags. On thinking about this work, I saw a lesson in this procedure. In the first talk I was to give in the new church, I made the connection and drew an analogy from when I was treating the field. I think people saw the point that preparation was and is so important to any project. The second point I referred to was that of the spiritual application, for if we were to make a difference in the area of the new church, then we had to be prepared spiritually for the task ahead. Lastly there is always the practical application. The church won't run itself, God needs hands, feet, time, means in order to advance His Kingdom. I see this as a principal in every Christian's life; if this were the case, the church would be in a different condition than what it finds itself in today.

What has this all got to do with my story? I have sought to share with you the practicalities of being able to reach out to help others along the way despite having a number of problems of my own; at the same time applying the lessons above i.e. planning, spiritual, practical based on my experiences when coming into contact with people and in my communications with others generally.

Later, in the first year of the new church opening I became a Deacon. This office deals principally with the practical issues involved within the church organisation. I counted it a privilege to serve in this way. I remember when we first opened the Sunday school in the new church, we were all astounded by the number of children that turned up. We had visited the neighbourhood prior to the opening event so as to gauge roughly how many we might expect on the day, but we hadn't envisaged so many. It was a good problem to have and it was just as well we got some help in, just in case. They were all needed! Further development took place within the house-groups once the church was up and running. We did get quite a number of new people from the estate and this was all very encouraging. Much work was carried out within the fellowship. God had answered prayer!

Sylvia and I stayed at the church for about twelve years, before moving on to a relative small work not very far from where we lived. They were building up the fellowship and the children's work. At that time, because I had been so involved with our previous church, I wanted to keep a 'low profile' and have a rest from all the activity that I and Sylvia had been involved in for the past twelve years. I certainly did not seek any kind of 'office', this, of course, was my intention! But I forgot, God takes a 'seat' next to one who says, 'I'll take a 'back seat'. He obviously had other ideas for me. I managed to keep my head down for about five months. I was going through a strange period in my life, maybe it was necessary for me to have a break of sorts. The dangerous thing about having a break can be that one can find it hard to get back into what normally motivates. I'm sure God knew all about what I was feeling; knew I needed a break. In the end I thought that I was being disobedient to what I was supposed to do and be. It's amazing how easy it is to be caught up in one's own ideas and concepts and miss out on what God is wanting your function to be, whether in a church situation or others. It's remembering that as a child of God, He has your best interests at heart and wants you to be a blessing to those around you for His glory, so being obedient is of paramount importance if we are to keep within His purposes. Of course there is no question of anyone being of themselves able to carry out any particular calling without the enabling of the Holy Spirit's anointing. To try to achieve any task worth achieving without His enabling is risky indeed. Sometimes we shy away from certain responsibilities because they may appear to be onerous or difficult and because of the fear and uncertainty of what might follow if we fail. If this is the case, then the possibility is that nothing would get done. We could find ourselves all standing around watching nothing getting done!

We had been at the church where we attended near our home for about five months. We heard that the treasurer of that church was stepping down; I sort of 'kept my head down' at that point. Shortly after the minister came to me to see if I could 'help' in the situation and become the new treasurer. The folk there knew that I'd had some experience in dealing with finance in my jobs. After some considerable thought, I agreed. I felt it was to be a firm commitment to the church. In such cases the office of treasurer didn't necessitate one to become a Deacon. Before long though, I found myself becoming a Deacon! So much for keeping my head down! I'm sure God has a sense of humour! Not only had I not been able to 'keep my head down' but within the first year I was to become the treasurer and a Deacon! Ha well! Bang goes that idea! But I'm glad God has all the best ideas. I found that there were quite a number of things to sort out, and I hoped that I could be of some help. Over the years my communication ability had become better and less stressful in that I was able to speak clearly on matters concerning the leadership of the church.

In the next few years, we as a church, had to consider the re-appraisal of the constitution. The Diaconate decided to re-write the constitution to include the matter of 'Biblical Eldership'. I must say that this matter was something that I had had on my mind for some time. Why I should had been the one to introduce this, I don't know, but there it was! I had been studying this for about three years and felt it was the right time to bring this matter before the church fellowship. Following a long period of consultation with the membership and a final paper being produced so that all the members could have an opportunity to comment, we decided to present it to a church meeting so that it could be included within the new constitution. At that meeting, it seemed good to us and the Holy Spirit to press ahead and include it as envisaged. There was much to learn in formulating the particular phraseology that was needful in this exercise.

These were times of challenge for me, as I never expected to become involved in such a matter. It was a steep learning curve, as I had never attempted anything like this before then. Eventually, much to my surprise, I was recognised as an Elder, along with another Brother at the same time. I did not anticipate this happening when I was studying the matter. Obviously the Lord had put this into my heart for a good reason. All the same, I felt unworthy to hold such office, yet God uses the most unlikely people to do His bidding. It's true, we cannot dictate to God whom He will use in His scheme of things, all we can do is to try to recognise what His plans are and act upon them. I remained at that church for about ten years until we moved into the town area, where it would be difficult to go backwards and forwards to where the church was.

We always seemed to be on the move! It was mainly to do with family requirements and the comings and goings of the children's schooling, growing up and wanting their own space, as it were, and getting married in the case of our eldest. We only had Paul at home then and a mad dog called 'Dino', a red setter, daft as a bag of nails but very good company. We moved down to the town centre and started attending the Baptist Church again where we first went when we came to Exmouth in the first place after moving from Ilford. After some time with them I was asked to stand again as a Deacon and served for just three years. During our stay at this church we had the opportunity to help a few of the people with 'special needs'. I felt that they were missing out on the true understanding of the act of Holy Communion. It became needful for them to get a basic appreciation of what it was all about. So I was led to speak to them about the matter and try to make them willing to have a session on the subject which they willingly did. They were absolutely thrilled that someone was taking an interest in them; as it was proved, it was very worthwhile and I had some very good responses. No longer would they sit through the service without understanding.

Some time after my wife's mother passed away, we decided that there was nothing to keep us in Exmouth. I felt I had done the work that was meant for me to do, so moved to Honiton, Devon. We asked the Lord to show us where He wanted us to be. After a month or so settling in, we visited the local Baptist church. We found the folk there to be very friendly and welcoming, which was a bit of a contrast to that from which we came. In fact it was different from any of our previous church experience. I suppose it might sound a bit sad to have to say this, but you can only judge as you find! We certainly were made to feel at home in this new situation. Without seeming to be too critical, some churches can be rather staid in their approach, both to the order of the services and their reception of visitors which can be a bit off-putting. I'm sure they are sincere in what they are about, but it can make all the difference in the first impressions that visitors get. For Honiton Baptist, there is no doubt about the welcome and the relaxed, but scriptural application to the services and the appeal to outsiders to come and join us in worship.

We began to settle into the fellowship, but at the same time I decided not to be in too much of a hurry to get too involved. I wanted to find out the direction the church was taking generally. I just committed this to God's leading. After about one year, I found myself being approached with regard to becoming a Deacon once again. I suppose that after what I have said before in this account about taking on an office, you could be forgiven for asking, why on earth did I allow my name to go forward for the Diaconate again. Well, only the Lord knows! He obviously had a plan once again and a particular task to fulfil. Sometimes in the Christian Life God tells you to do something without us necessarily having to know the whole picture, all we need to do is to obey Him. Why? Because He knows what is best for us. That is the reason why I let my name go forward at that point. As it turned out, there were several matters, without going into detail, which had been left undone in previous years, which needed to be completed; including the re-construction and organising of the constitution including also the addition of the Eldership clause. When looking back I can see why the Lord wanted Sylvia and I to be part of this fellowship. Not because I was any more capable than others, I'm sure that if I hadn't been there, someone else would had been involved. God intended that this church should make progress to become more effective in its witness. So it pleased the Lord to use me in the situation as well as others in this process, for which I am very grateful to God for.

When God begins a work in a person whether me or anyone else, He goes on to complete it. I wish to thank all those who have helped me in so many ways along the way. Many of the tasks which have been performed, would not had been possible without that help.

Chapter 10

The point of it all

Some people might be tempted to say, "Why bother to write this account of my experiences?" I suppose it's a fair question, if posed from a position of never having had any kind of disability, disfigurement of any kind, or mobility problems. We can include in this, psychological problems or the feelings of inadequacy in any situation. There are so many scenarios out there that would warrant some sort of help or counsellor expertise. My feelings about all this when deciding to write about my life were that, if I could help someone to know better how to cope with these experiences, and come out the other side more able to face the many obstacles that life puts in our way sometimes, then I am happy, to some degree, to lay myself open and share my experiences. Perhaps someone may pick up on the way I dealt with some of the problems highlighted in this story to the extent that it helps others to come to terms with the challenges they face from time to time. If it has that effect, then I would have achieved what I set out to do in the first place. For this reason I feel it has been a worthwhile exercise. This account is mainly aimed at those who have or are experiencing any of the above difficulties, but not exclusively! There are many who appear not to have any problems of the sort I have described, yet, none-the-less, have needs that cannot be readily recognised until one gets talking to them.

We live in a world that is always in such a rush that some have not the time to stop and listen to those whose needs are less obvious. Everyone has some kind of need! Nobody is exempt from trials and difficulties in their lives. Look at it this way, if you spot a flower that is suffering because of disease, lack of water or environment issues, wouldn't you try to remedy the problem by meeting the particular need where you can? Of course you would! But this would be dependant on whether you had the time to stop and observe and take action in the first place. If you hadn't the "time to stop and stare" then nothing would be solved. It's the same with human needs as well as animals' needs. We all live in this world, what a better place it would be, if we cared for one another! Given the opportunity to develop and flourish, those who are disabled or inflicted in any way could be in a position to help others who are suffering in turn to be able to flourish. I have known many folk who we would call disabled become expert in many different fields, because they had received help along the way. I have learned never to take for granted, or judge a person by the way they look, walk, or talk and conduct themselves generally. One can be so wrong in these situations. It can be a great mistake and embarrassment if one is assumed to be 'not quite with it', whatever 'it' is, merely because of external characteristics. I'm sure there are those who present a 'perfect' image in appearance 'as seen on TV' have needs which cannot easily be identified; they too need help. There are many 'out there' who are willing to spend time with those less fortunate than themselves, thank God for them.

There are many also who would be happy to help others, if only they knew how they may help! In many cases where some person attempts to help, they do so in a slightly condescending way, as though the person they are helping finds it difficult to understand what you are saying. This can be a mistake! When a person has a problem with speech or mobility, it doesn't necessarily mean they are unintelligent or something else is wrong. There are, of course, some cases where this might be the situation, but we must exercise care in such cases. I speak from personal experience from when I was between the ages of 5-20 years of age. I could not speak clearly and often the reaction was as described above. This treatment is often present when dealing with younger people. They automatically assume that there is something wrong with the brain in such cases. It's a matter of 'education' I hasten to add! Not all youngsters have this reaction, some are very good at communicating with those affected by disabilities.

Where people we meet do have the tendency to speak-down to us, our best response is to be assertive and positive. This disarms them, their attitude changes and you can watch it happen! You will be surprised how often this takes place, and when it does and you remain positive, observe how your own confidence grows. In some cases, the person who is addressing you finds it difficult to look directly at you, especially if you have a facial disfigurement. It's not because they don't like you! It is more likely they don't know how to respond, or what to do and say. Once this barrier has been broken down, life gets to become a little more bearable both for them and you. It is quite a natural reaction to a situation where some imperfection exists. It's not your fault, not the fault of the one speaking to you, it's just how life is!

I can tell you, people who have any of these imperfections, have a lot to offer to an imperfect world, and there are many who are extremely talented, which the world cannot do without. So if you are one of those people who has experienced, or are experiencing imperfection, disability or any other complaint in your life, then I would say to you, "You have some talents, develop them, use them, for yourselves and the benefit of others. The world needs you and your abilities." Yes, your abilities. It's a matter of turning disabilities into abilities, no matter how seemingly insignificant. Let us accentuate those things that will bring benefit to those around us, rather than keep them locked up in the prison of our minds. My great desire is - I'm sure it is yours, is to make our mark on society, not to be pushed into the corner as insignificant, where nothing happens. Let us make it happen! Whatever the arena of operations happens to be, let us not be afraid to stand up and say "Here I am. I'm a person just like everyone else!"

I am always impressed when I see those taking part in the Para Olympics, observing how they have overcome their limitations. Some of the seemingly impossible difficulties have been brushed aside through sheer hard work and determination, patience, tenacity and will-power, in order to gain those accolades of gold, silver and bronze. These people deserve the recognition and admiration of their peers. They consider their participation in these activities as making a statement that they are 'as good as everyone else', and their disabilities are no reason to be left behind! Put it down to sheer determination and guts, that they can rise above their limitations - there is no way that they are going to be left out of the 'grand picture' of human endeavour. I suppose, what I am saying is, we can and must come to terms with, and rise above our deficiencies; we can treat them like hurdles in an obstacle race. The approach to these hurdles has to be calculated, practised, tackled and then overcome. All this applies to the different types of imperfections and limitations that people suffer in life, they can deal with any disability and change them to become abilities.

Everyone has a hidden talent somewhere! It is when we fail to recognise this fact that the lack of confidence rears its ugly head. No matter how small or insignificant this talent or 'gift' might be, it should be recognised and used. Where we are disabled or otherwise, let us nurture, develop and shape that gift, whatever it be, until it becomes a useful tool in the hands of its possessor for the good of others.

There are so many tools we can use these days to help those who are afflicted in any way to be able to make an impact on society. If anyone is unable to walk, then there are the means to get around. If any are unable to talk, then there are computers that can help you express what you are thinking and give one a voice. It doesn't matter how long it takes to get your message keyed in. There are folk who are willing to help you in such circumstances. Tools like these open up a whole new world of communication whereby one can get over the message that one is trying to convey. If it's a case of disfigurement of some kind, it comes back to what I have suggested in this account, dependant on people's reactions to our looks; let us be assertive and positive and we will find folk will ignore that aspect of us. Underneath that façade of imperfection is a real person trying to get out. I speak from personal experience of this and how I was ultimately able to deal with it. This is why I am sharing this with you the reader, so that you will know where I am coming from and that my intention here is to encourage people who have these problems in their lives. So I sincerely hope that what I have expressed up to now in the story will be the source of real triumph over this type of adversity. With the help of others we can do so much more than we expect.

When you think about it, there is little we cannot achieve if we have the kind of determination to succeed. It may be only small things, small goals at first, nobody is counting! Can I encourage you? If you have not already found the inspiration or desire to get started on something that has been on your mind for ages, and you've wondered whether you are able to carry it out, Get started on it today! You will be surprised once you have begun, and will ask yourself "Why on earth didn't I start on it before?" It doesn't matter what type of disability you may be experiencing, you can work within the limits of your capability. Yes, getting the help you need from others who are willing to give you assistance, using the 'tools' available and thereby turning your disabilities into 'abilities' as I have said before.

Remember, I wrote before, I had to learn to speak three times due to the number and character of my operations. This called for a lot of hard work on my part; no one could help me in this, I had to work on it myself. There were some points at which I would have given it up as a bad job - had I done that and sat back feeling sorry for myself, nothing would had been achieved. I took the view that I would never be able to speak clearly or to make anything of myself! Instead I realised that I had to persevere if I was to be able to get work and communicate with others more effectively. There is an old saying: "God helps those who help themselves". I know this to be true in reality.

Although I found that helping myself was not the easy option, once I began to get to grips with what was required, in order for people to take me seriously, I pressed on in the hope that one day I would get to the point where people could understand me without too much difficulty and without me having to repeat everything that I said. I was very fortunate to have people around me who would urge me on and encourage me when I was flagging a bit, after all, I was only human and would often make mistakes, or rush things a bit and get it all slightly wrong. There were times when I was due to speak to a certain group of people, then at the last minute I would be tempted to chicken out because I was very nervous as to how I was to cope with the situation. In the end I did manage to keep my appointment and things went alright. This, of course, happens to lots of people that have no impediments at all, so I shouldn't had been surprised at this. In these circumstances we have to give ourselves 'a good talking to!' or someone else would have the pleasure! To come to the point, I had to learn to 'speak- up'. Had I not persevered with my talking, I could never have been able to hold down some of the jobs that I was later to be doing. "I'm no different to anyone else" I kept telling myself, and sometimes I needed others to convince me of this. On occasion I would get a 'right dressing down' from my friends if I began to feel sorry for myself. They would observe in me a lack of confidence and they would try to make me see reason. I thank God they did!

I do appreciate that some of the things I have been sharing with you may seem a little harsh, and I know some of you have acute problems to deal with. I am quite sure that you don't just want sympathy for your condition, there is plenty of that out there! On the contrary, I'm sure you would prefer constructive, practical and worthwhile help to improve your situation, am I right? I did, and still do need help sometimes. There is a great deal of difference between sympathy and empathy. With the first, it's mainly to convey the feeling of pity or tenderness towards the one who is suffering pain or discomfort, but without the ability or experience to be able to help the person's condition. On the other hand the person who has empathy, which is the ability to identify themselves mentally, because they have had the same or similar experience as the one who is being helped. It certainly does help if the person you are speaking to is, or has been, in the same position as oneself.

Why have I shared this story with you? Let me first assure you it is not because I am particularly clever! I'm not. I am just an ordinary person who has had to cope with a number of fairly significant physical problems since I was born back in 1938. These problems have had to be overcome, otherwise no progress could had been made that would have brought purpose and meaning to my life. The point of it all, was to encourage anyone who has experienced any of the shortcomings, whether physical, mental or any other disabilities that might had prevented one from living a normal life, to know that there is a way to overcome to some degree some of the side-effects of such difficulties, and to realise that there are people who can help in the situation. I came to the conclusion, that if

I can face the world with the help of those who have been by my side, and in turn I have been able to help my peers who have suffered in any way, then that is what life is all about! There's part of a song that goes something like this, not necessarily exact words:-
"If I could help somebody
Then my life would not had been in vain"
If we can live out this expression of care towards each other, then certainly it would be worthwhile!

I have learned that in the dictionary the word 'can't' does not exist. There is no such word! Some say that miracles do not exist, but I would contend with that! With God 'all things are possible' but miracles take a little longer! No! I correct myself there, miracles can be instantaneous! I would say - if you had been able to see me at birth, and observe the way I looked then, and compare this with the way I look now, I believe you would agree with my conclusions, a miracle has taken place. True it was over a period of time. But when you consider that all the surgeons can do is to carry out the operations, it is down to the Almighty to actually carry out the healing of the flesh. That's why I call it a miracle! It was over a period on time where patience had to rule the day, the months and the years, but sometimes in our lives we have to make haste slowly, to coin a phrase.

What ever your disabilities, it's all about changing them into abilities. A blind man or woman can see a lot further by audio than someone who can see with their eyes but not with their mind. Someone who is deaf can listen very intently and respond very correctly, by means of the written word or visual means, compared to the person who is able to listen, but does not do so. It's not the outward appearance that matters, but what goes on inside that makes all the difference!

I place my picture on the front Title page as witness to what God has done through the medical means which He used to bring healing and purpose to my life.

                        A miracle! none-the-less

My Positive Conclusion

How the years have flown! It's 72 years since I made my grand entrance into this world. Or perhaps 'not so grand'. None of us know how long we have still to reside here and the time comes for me to lay aside all the effort in trying to speak clearly and not have to worry about my looks any more. In heaven it won't matter what we look like! The main thing is I'll be there. If we are believers in what Jesus has achieved for us, that is all that matters. No! I won't get my wings, I won't need them!

I want to be open and honest before you who are reading this story. It may be you have not come from a background of physical imperfection and /or disabilities of any kind, or indeed, have had no experience of any of these conditions. It makes no difference, whatever your experience, God treats us as individuals. I know one thing for sure, that God has always been with me, even though I have not always been aware of it. I certainly would not have survived those years of trauma, especially in the early years of my life without His help. My belief in Him has been my experience. I have shared this with you in the hope that it has encouraged and strengthened you in your life's journey.

I have met many people who tell you that they do not need any 'crutches' (religion) in their lives. Well, I agree with them! I don't need a religious 'crutch' in my life because I have a faith that sustains me, and that faith is in the Almighty God of creation, who made me, 'just as I am'. My dependence and well-being was upon Him, and if He cannot help me, I don't stand much chance of success whether in this life or the next, that is if we believe that there is a life to come! I would find it difficult to believe that this life is all there is. We surely cannot believe that we go through all this life, with all its ups and downs, its problems, whether physical, environmental, or whatever, only to be left with nothing. What's the purpose in that? If I believed this was the case, I would give up now. I can tell you there is someone who is concerned about our well-being, more especially, about our spiritual and eternal well-being. At the end of the day, our allotted time span on this earth is not that long is it? So let us make the most of it by caring for one another, by doing our best to use the gifts that God has given to each one of us in order to alleviate the sufferings of others and bring help and comfort to them.

It's good to know that one day we will be able to lay aside this rather imperfect tent in which we live, with all its problems, pains and aches, both perceived and imaginary or real, its sadness and joys, its limitations and let-downs, its successes and failures. These things will be left behind when we meet our maker, to be remembered no more.

There are many people who just do not believe that there is anything that follows this life. I must say to quote a phrase from the bible "If we have hope in this life only, then we are of men/women most miserable". How people can believe that they can survive in a world without hope of a future, I can't imagine! My quest is, that they may come to realise there is someone to whom we can turn, and His name is Jesus. It is He alone who is able to give us the hope that the world so badly needs. What constitutes happiness? Good looks, the ability to communicate, wealth and riches, status in life, popularity, and every other thing that makes life easier? We all know that these things are temporary and can easily be destroyed or taken from us. Material things are just things! We can't take them with us, there is no removal van following the hearse in our send off. All we can do is leave something for our kin, as long as the government doesn't get it first! So where does this all leave us? Is there something missing in our lives? Or do we go through life giving the appearance of success and everything going for us, but inwardly we are craving for fulfilment and a point to our lives? This is why so many so-called successful people end up psychologically and mentally affected by all the pressures of keeping up with the Joneses. They present an outer veneer of confidence without having the wherewithal to actually cope because of pride. Because of pride this type of person refuses to open up to others to share their misgivings over many things and thereby miss out on any counsel that may be available. Often it is they who need the help more than those we think need help. So it is not just physical shortcomings that affect people's lives, it is also mental, spiritual or psychological conditions that come into play. As I said before, "Sometimes a person looks fine and near perfect, as seen on TV, but underneath there can be real problems".

I hope this account of my experiences will serve to encourage you the reader and enable you to strike out in greater confidence in all your dealings with others, especially in the areas of communication. I make no apology for sharing with you the source of the help I received in the light of my faith and belief.

Michael Chering
23rd June 2010

Lightning Source UK Ltd.
Milton Keynes UK
UKOW040713220312

189381UK00002B/1/P